Make your own
BEER *and* CIDER

Make your own
BEER *and* CIDER

PAUL PEACOCK

SPRING HILL

Published by Spring Hill

Spring Hill is an imprint of How To Books Ltd
Spring Hill House, Spring Hill Road,
Begbroke, Oxford, OX5 1RX, United Kingdom
Tel: (01865) 375794 Fax: (01865) 379162
info@howtobooks.co.uk
www.howtobooks.co.uk

How To Books greatly reduce the carbon footprint of their books by sourcing their
typesetting and printing in the UK.

British Library Cataloguing in Publication Data
A catalogue record for this book is available from the British Library

ISBN: 978 1 905862 62 7

Text illustrations by Rebecca Peacock
Produced for How To Books by Deer Park Productions, Tavistock
Typeset by TW Typesetting, Plymouth, Devon
Printed and bound in Great Britain by MPG Books Group, Bodmin, Cornwall

NOTE: The material contained in this book is set out in good faith for general
guidance and no liability can be accepted for loss or expense incurred as a result of
relying in particular circumstances on statements made in this book. Laws and
regulations may be complex and liable to change, and readers should check the
current position with the relevant authorities before making personal arrangements.

CONTENTS

Introduction **1**
How to use this book 2
Why brew at home? 4
The importance of beer 5
Different types of home brew 7
The biology of yeast 8
What yeast needs to do its job 11
The chemistry of fermentation 13
The biology of barley 15

1 **What you need to know to brew beer and cider** **17**
How brewing used to be done 18
How to make the best beer in the world 20
Modern brewing explained 21
Finding out the alcohol content of beer 28
Beer recipes and how to follow them 32
Variations in recipes 37
Sterilising your equipment 39
Bottling your beer 44

2 **Understanding what goes into a pint of beer** **47**
The basic fundamentals explained 48
Understanding the difference between base and
    non-base malts 49
Using whole grains 52
Using hops 52

Putting it all together: making your beer   55
Making fun beer   56

3   How to make beer from a kit   **60**
Find yourself a good brew shop   60
Sterilising your equipment   61
The contents of the brew kit   62
Making beer from your brew kit   64
Modifying a beer kit   68
Making your own beer kit   71

4   Making pale ale and bitter   **74**
India pale ale   76
Making pale ale   76
Making easy bitter beer from extract   77
Making bitter beer   78
Making a simple pale ale using extract   80
Making pale ale   81
Making India pale ale   82
Making light pale ale   83
Making wheat beer   84
Making all grain wheat beer   85

5   Making mild beer   **87**
Nut brown ale   89
Making a really simple mild   89
Making brown ale   91
Making mild beer with chocolate malt   93
Making easy Guinness   94

6   Making stout and strong ales   **96**
Original gravity   97

Making porter using malt extract 97
Making stout 98
Making milk stout 99
Making a Mackeson clone 100
Making barley wine 101
Making barley wine from extract 102
Making honeyed beer 103

7   Making lager **105**
The characteristics of lager 106
Making a really easy lager 107
Making lager using Saaz hops 108
Making lager using flaked maize 109
Making dark lager 110

8   Making cider and perry **112**
Understanding apples for cider 114
Making your cider sweet or dry 116
Traditional small-scale cider making 116
Making rough cider 118
Cheating apple wine 121
More complex cider recipes 122
Making cider using the freezer 122
More cider recipes 124
Fruited ciders 125
Making perry 126

9   Making root beer, ginger beer and small beer **131**
Carrot beer 132
Carrot wine 132
Potato beer 134
Potato wine 135

Mixed-root dry white wine 137
Ginger beer 138
Small beer 140

10 Making true home brew **142**
Growing hops 143
Growing barley 145
Growing apples 147

Brewing glossary **151**

Index 159

INTRODUCTION

Like the pubs that are exactly halfway between towns in northern England, this little book is a halfway house. It provides you, the reader, with all the skills and knowledge necessary to make beer and cider, and a few other drinks besides. As a starting point, we'll take a look at the beer kit, and then look at how to create a really excellent pint by modifying and experimenting. Then the book goes on to present a number of extraction recipes (where extracted malt is used) and mashing recipes (where grains and malted barley grains are used – also known as whole grain). While you're at it, how about having a go at making cider? You'll find recipes for that here too. It's worth noting that when it comes to cider making, the apples are everything, and so we'll look at the various mixtures of apples needed to create certain cider types. And if you think cider is a child's drink, try saying that in any Rugby Club in the south-east of England! Just to get you started, try my turbo cider recipe, which is made from apple juice you can buy in the supermarket!

The idea is that any reader, even someone with no brewing experience at all, can progress to the point where they are confident to pick up one of the myriad beer recipes available (some of which have no step-by-step instructions) and work out what to do.

In essence, this book signposts the route from beer and cider consumption to beer and cider production on the household scale, in the hope that its readers will find again the complete joy of a simple life lubricated by simple pleasures.

HOW TO USE THIS BOOK

Most authors want you to enjoy their books. Well I don't! I want you to enjoy my beer! So flit around this book, find recipes you fancy making and get stuck in. Make mistakes, do the wrong thing, but get stuck in.

Just to get you going, pop along to your local brew shop and show him this book. Most people don't believe this will work, but have a go. (If you happen to go to my favourite brew shop, Spitting Feathers in Bolton, ask for a discount. You might not get one, but you can try . . .)

Ask for this list:

- 1 fermenting bin with lid (let's not get involved with airlocks yet) 22.5 litres capacity

- 1 best bitter kit

- 1.5 kg pale malt extract

- 1 plastic tube for siphoning the beer off the lees (called racking)

- Some sterilising solution – see the section on sterilising on page 39, but you need to do it to the fermenting bin, the lid and the equipment.

- 1 paddle – unless you are really poor and need to use a wooden spoon from the kitchen, you use this to mix the brew at the mixing stage.

What to do with it:

- Ignore the instructions.

- Put about 10 litres of tap water in the fermenting bin.

- Use boiling water to get the wort (sugary liquid – beer juice) out of the can.

- Add the malt extract (don't worry about sugar). Stir and top up to 22.5 litres with tap water.

- Give it another stir and leave for 24 hours.

- Add the yeast, put the lid on and place in a moderately warm room.

- 12–15 days later you will have beer.

You will notice a grey solid at the bottom of the bucket. It looks like the worst bit of Blackpool Beach on sewage day before they cleaned it up. You need to use the plastic tube to siphon the nice beer from the nasty lees at the bottom.

You could use another sterile fermenting bin, or a keg or bottles to put the beer in – even I couldn't drink 22.5 litres just through a plastic tube – but remember to sterilise everything you are putting your beer into.

It won't be the best beer in the world – but it will be ten times better than most of the stuff you buy in cans in the supermarket and it will be a lot cheaper.

So, now you have entered the mysterious world of brewing beer!

WHY BREW AT HOME?

Thirst is a terrible thing!

My first memories of home brew came from Fred Astaire. He had two hobbies in life: ballroom dancing (hence the nickname) and brewing beer. It was very bad beer, and he used to very kindly leave a couple of bottles each week for my father, who would lift them to the light as though he knew what he was looking for and then pour it down the sink.

I beat my father to it one day, had a drink, and poured the rest down the sink. Perhaps, at eight years of age I was not sufficiently mature enough to make a reasonable judgement, but it tasted awful. Nothing like the beer I had drunk at my uncle's pub which, although the rest of the pub smelt of vinegar, was warm and strangely adult, the very first thing I had ever found to taste different between the front and the back of my mouth.

Real, or perhaps I should say 'good', home brewing does not produce the almost poisonous flavours of the concoctions of yesteryear. Probably most people will recoil at the memory of some brew or other produced in the back kitchen, in too warm an environment, using sucrose as a base, and a syrupy beer kit as a wort.

Beer made at home, beer made from raw materials, and even kit beers given a little care and cleanliness, would not be out of place in a really good pub. Home-made kit beer can be stunning, given the right ingredients, but beer made from raw materials would win prizes compared to the gassy liquid found in cans and bottles around the supermarkets.

If you want real quality beer, go to a real ale pub, or make your own.

THE IMPORTANCE OF BEER

Until recent years, wheat was a difficult crop to grow. The further north you were, the harder it became to produce wheat fit enough to make bread from the grain. Consequently, much of our wheat comes from the US, where it is easier and cheaper to produce.

Barley, however, grows well in the UK climate – even as far north as Scotland. Barley bread is not much more than pap, but the malting barley made beer – which is far more nutritious than any other food. Firstly, purified with alcohol, beer is safe to drink. Secondly it is high in carbohydrates, and vitamins.

Whereas bread is the staff of life, beer is the stuff to wash it down. When reformers, who were concerned about the supposed 'wantoness' of the beer drinking classes, introduced tea as a way of drinking safe liquid, they unfortunately had no understanding of nutrition. The reformers were actually more interested in morals than health, and a large number of people suffered malnutrition after signing the pledge. Without the nutrients they had previously got from beer, they died for want of proper food! The ragged poor might have been fit for heaven, and it was a good job – they were visiting it all the quicker.

More than just beer

William Cobbett was to self sufficiency what Delia Smith is to cooking. The Member of Parliament for Oldham in Lancashire was incensed about the way ordinary people were being brought into poverty. In 1833 he published a book, *Cottage Economy*, detailing how ordinary people had stopped brewing beer in their homes.

Essentially, between the years of 1780 and 1820, the government increased tax on malted barley and hops. In 1780 nearly every home brewed its own beer; by 1820, no one did – instead they had to go to ale houses in order to buy from the breweries who owned the barley, the fields, the hop gardens, the brew houses and the beer they produced. At this time people's pay had changed from real money, coins of the realm, to paper money – often little more than tickets to be used in their employers' shops. With this monopoly handed to them on a plate, brewers became very rich indeed, and they continue to be some of the most successful businesses in the world.

In his book, Cobbett showed people how to brew beer and bake bread, but it was too late, the nation had become enslaved to the baker and the publican.

So, why not thwart the vested interest and become rich? Making your own beer might not bring in any money, but you will have wonderful beer to drink: chemical-free beer, cheaper beer than the cheapest you can buy (I can make it for around 30p a pint) and more to the point, the best beer than anyone could ever taste.

Please drink sensibly!

Beer brewed at home is not really for continuous consumption. The idea of home brewers being gouty middle-aged men with red noses, beer bellies and skin like a corpse is horrifying.

You also have to remember that home brew is often a lot stronger than the commercial stuff, so drink accordingly. A quart a day would seem just about right, which means you would need a three-week brew cycle to have a permanent supply!

DIFFERENT TYPES OF HOME BREW

Beer kits

Kits are much more simple than you might think! The main thing about this way of brewing is that it is easy, so long as you get the cleanliness part right. Everything should be sterilised before use and the brewing beer should be kept at a temperature of between 18 and 21°C for a few weeks until it is ready to drink.

Using a kit is not the cheapest way to brew per pint, but it is the way most people actually brew for the first time. You don't need much in the way of equipment – just a pan and a fermentation vessel can be enough.

There are lots of different beers to choose from, and you can set off five gallons (22.5 litres) in a couple of hours.

Brewing from malt extract

Essentially, brew kits are made from an extracted wort which is sometimes not much more than malt extract. You can buy malt extract in many forms, including as a syrup in a tin or bottle, or dried. Dilute this and then boil with hops before cooling and fermenting and you get a decent beer.

The hops are there to add bitterness to the beer and it does preserve the beer in some measure too.

Mashing or all grain brewing

This is the business of brewing from raw materials. Sugar and other substances are released from the malted grain when soaked in warm water. This gives you a wort – the fundamental liquid for brewing. This is boiled with hops, and perhaps other natural substances, to create your brewing liquid.

Mashing is probably the cheapest way, pint for pint, to make beer at home, but it is also the best in terms of quality. Yes, you do need more equipment, but this can be used again and again.

Making cider

In its simplest form, making cider is little more complicated than adding juice to a barrel. Of course, there are always exceptions to the rule, but in general cider making – real top of the range cider making – is not difficult at all.

Yes you can!

Don't worry! If you can cook a Sunday roast dinner, you can brew beer or cider. Brewing is not rocket science, it is not difficult in any way, and is likely to be one of the most rewarding occupations you can find.

THE BIOLOGY OF YEAST

Sit down for a long time and your legs start to brew

Perhaps it's my age ... When I used to play rugby, a long time ago, I would be three-quarters through the game and would have to stop for a horrid pain in my left leg. It was as though someone had put some kind of medieval clamp on my muscle and screwed it tight. Then, for good measure, someone else – obviously an invisible someone with malice – would take an equally invisible blow torch and pass it to and fro over my leg.

The resulting pain was incredible, and the game had to be stopped until the physio had rubbed the horror away, a process that as I approached the end of my playing career, made me scream loudly and embarrassingly.

The formation of cramp has a lot to do with the production of alcohol. When there is a lot of oxygen available to my legs, I can run and tackle, score tries and scrum with the best of them. My muscles take the available oxygen from blood and use it to respire. This gave me the energy to take the ball at the back of a scrum, on the halfway line, run 50 yards, sidestep two people and score a try in 2007, on my 50th birthday.

The energy used by my legs came from the breakdown of sugar in my bloodstream, using oxygen to complete the job. The result was an increase of carbon dioxide, which I had to get rid of by bending over and breathing hard like a dying hen, which at my age was the only method that really worked.

Twenty minutes of hard playing later I would be on the floor, rolling in agony. What had happened was the amount of oxygen available to my muscles was decreasing, but because the game of rugby demanded I continued performing, I ran on. My muscles, in order to compensate for my lack of fitness, have a fantastic trick up their sleeves (or is it up their trousers?).

Instead of respiring normally, muscles can switch how they retrieve the energy from the sugar in my blood. Using an anaerobic pathway to get energy from sugar, they do the job without oxygen at all. The only problem being that this method also produces another substance called lactic acid, and as that builds up in the muscles, the side effect is horribly painful cramp.

Yeast doesn't play rugby

The amazing thing about yeast cells is, like us, they can switch how they respire from aerobic to anaerobic. Tiny yeast cells give off carbon dioxide from ordinary respiration. The energy released gives the cells the ability to reproduce themselves, to grow and divide very rapidly. However, having used up all the oxygen in a closed container, they then switch their mode of respiration to anaerobic.

Respiring without oxygen, like my tired legs, has a side effect in the yeast. Instead of producing lactic acid, the poor yeast cell produces an even more deadly substance – alcohol. This is exited from the cell into the liquid it is growing in. Within a couple of weeks the alcohol level in the beer, wine or cider, has built up to proportions that kill the yeast cells, and fermentation stops. And by a series of clever tricks, we enjoy the results of their microscopic demise.

Brewing needs both

When we brew beer or cider, we actually utilize both methods of respiration. In the wort (the term we use for beer juice that we have made by one method or another) there is a lot of oxygen dissolved in the water. There is also a lot of sugar. When we add yeast, it has the ideal conditions, assuming the temperature is favourable, for rapid reproduction. The yeast multiplies at least ten-fold until all the oxygen has been used up. In brewing your own home-made beer or wine or cider, you need this stage. It is an important step to build up the amount of yeast in the brew. Then, once the oxygen is used up, the little cells start to burp out alcohol as they switch to anaerobic respiration, making your beer juice worth drinking.

The exciting thing is that they are also giving out carbon dioxide, and for every bubble you see in the brewing liquid, you get exactly the same number of molecules of alcohol – it is a 1:1 process.

You need the oxygen to give the yeast a kick-start to build up their numbers, and you need the oxygen-free conditions to turn your drink into something alcoholic.

When yeast uses oxygen to release energy from sugar the process is called respiration. When it switches to anaerobic methods, the process is called fermentation.

Isn't it a good job?

The thought occurs to me that a mistake of evolution could have made life quite interesting. Maybe, if our muscles produced alcohol instead of lactic acid, like yeast, ten press-ups would be like having a glass of beer. You could get a bit tiddly during a gym session or get totally smashed on a marathon. The Olympics would be quite a different spectacle!

Perhaps cramp is not a bad thing after all.

WHAT YEAST NEEDS TO DO ITS JOB

Yeast is a simple, single-celled fungus, and there are many varieties. Some cider-making methods use wild yeast, on the surface of apples, to ferment the sugar in the juice, in barrels. Most wine making uses specific yeasts for clarets, generic whites and reds, champagne, some rosé wine and other more specialist wines. There are also specific yeasts for brewing beer and making bread.

All yeasts have fundamental needs, and then we have some equally fundamental requirements from yeast that it is important to take note of.

Temperature

Yeast works best in the region of 18–21°C. Any cooler, and the fermentation will be slow; any warmer and it might be too rapid, something we will touch upon later.

When you start yeast off, it is important that you get it warm so that it starts to reproduce, which doesn't always happen at cooler temperatures.

Often, when you are struggling to get the brew going, it is temperature that is mostly at fault. Leave the wort at room temperature, and give it a few hours to warm up, and you will probably have no difficulty in getting the yeast off to a good start.

Water

Really, this is obvious: you cannot make beer or any other beverage without water. However, since all living things need water to live, keeping yeast dry is the best way to preserve it. The yeast forms spores and cocoons itself when dry and will keep for a long time.

Oxygen

As we have already discussed the complexities of yeast and its respiration methods, we only need to state here that, if you are keeping live wet yeast (fresh yeast), you will need to ensure it has oxygen to continue to live. However, there are very few reasons for keeping yeast cultures from one batch of beer to the next.

People do keep bread yeast, called sourdough, in this way, and I suppose the temptation to inoculate a new brew with yeast from an ongoing brew can be tempting – but there are reasons (see below) why we should not.

Vitamin C

Bought yeasts often have vitamin C in the packet. Yeast, like humans, cannot make vitamin C but needs it to live. Most fruits have some vitamin C content, but this isn't really guaranteed. And if you have a large brew going, you will often have to add more.

Sometimes this is done by adding a tablet. From time to time I have started yeast going with some rosehip syrup, which is both sweet and packed in Vitamin C.

THE CHEMISTRY OF FERMENTATION

Every schoolboy used to know the old-fashioned formula for the breakdown of sugar to give carbon dioxide, water and energy. It used to be the 'O'-level question for balancing chemical equations.

Like everything at school, the things we learned were not really accurate and it was always more complex than that. So it goes with brewing.

The starting point for respiration in more or less all cells is glucose, and yeast is no exception. Glucose is basically a ring molecule, but most sugars are combinations of this ring molecule. And there are other ring molecules, resembling glucose, that are also classed as sugars. They are called saccharides.

Glucose is a monosaccharide, consisting of a single ring. Lactose and maltose are disaccharides, consisting of two rings.

Sucrose, the white sugar we refine from beet or cane and use in the home, is a disaccharide made up of a ring of glucose and a ring of fructose.

Which sugar to use

The reason for all this chemistry is to help you to understand a simple fact. For yeast to use sucrose, it has to break it down first. This does not happen cleanly, and a number of different molecules result that the yeast cells try to respire. Some of these, in the absence of oxygen, won't break down at all. The result is a number of flavours so reminiscent of home brew. It tastes amateurish, not like professionally brewed beer or cider.

The answer is to use glucose in all your brewing, especially beer. Often cider is made using just apples, and wine is often made using just fruit, but using glucose in beer gives a much improved, more professional flavour.

If yeast is microscopic how do you know what's going on?

If you can't see what the yeast is doing, and more specifically if you can't see what kinds of yeast are in your brew, how do you know there is nothing in there that will poison you?

After all, sugar and water is an ideal medium for growing microbes of all kinds. The answer is, you can't. But of course, once the final brew is finished and you have 5% or more alcohol concentration, this is enough to keep your drink safe and preserved.

It is important that you do not allow spurious microbes to spoil your beer or any other fermented product. Scrupulous cleanliness, excellent sterilization techniques and being sure to use only perfect ingredients are all important in brewing. This is not a lesson to learn by experience, you have to get it right every time.

THE BIOLOGY OF BARLEY

Barley is a northern grass, or cereal, which will produce a crop in fairly mild, but not necessarily warm conditions. Barley, along with oats, can be grown in Scotland where wheat is not so common a crop.

Moreover, barley is an all-round crop grown in most parts of the world, and has distinctive characteristics common to all continents.

The way the seeds fill the head is important for beer brewing. Barley is classified into two-row, four-row and six-row barley, according to how many rows of seeds fill the head of corn. (The word corn is used here in the English parlance as meaning grain. All grains can be called corn in English, but in the US corn usually refers to maize.)

Two-row barley

This seems to be the most ancient of the barleys, being in cultivation some 5,000 years ago. There are references to it in ancient Egyptian writing, and indeed, its use in making beer.

This is the barley of choice for European beer manufacture, as it has a good, malty flavour.

Four-row barley

A genetic change which is common in grass, the doubling of the number of chromosomes , made four-row and six-row barley. Some people think four-row barley is simply a special derivative of six-row barley. Four-row barley is not used in the production of beer.

Six-row barley

This is sometimes favoured in American beers for the complexity of its sugars and consequently of the flavours in the beer.

It might be difficult to obtain in the UK, but it is recognised by the number of twisted grains. Six rows of grain in a head makes them twist and overlap, whereas there is plenty of room in two-row barley for the grains to grow out normally, without having to twist to fit in the available space.

CHAPTER 1

WHAT YOU NEED TO KNOW TO BREW BEER AND CIDER

Robinson Crusoe had it easy! In the story, he was shipwrecked and the contents of his ship, minus the crew, floated neatly on shore for him to use during his long stay. Presumably he had brewing equipment, for how would over four years alone on an island be bearable without beer?

The rest of us have to buy the equipment, which needn't be too much really. Essentially all you need is a container to brew in, another to make the wort, some way of sterilising the containers, and a means of keeping the air out of the system. Of course, you also need a means of drinking the liquid once produced.

When I was at university I spent a year with some very famous room-mates. At least, they were famous when I joined them. The reason for their fame was brown ale. They had, in the kitchen, a microbrewery that produced brown ale. Students from all across the campus would come and purchase a jug full, and we had a regular stream knocking on our door most nights.

The brewer was a pharmacology student, Chris, who had done a course on brewing. His system was simple. A series of large dustbins contained the brewing liquid (there were six of them altogether). The beer was brewed, then siphoned into a series of jugs and bottles as people arrived. He used a black bin bag over the neck of the bin, held in place by the lid. His complete kit consisted of some dustbins, a lot of sterilising tablets, a piece of plastic tubing, a few spoons, a large pan for making his wort, and a hydrometer, 'because you have to have everything proper', he said.

So it is possible to brew with very little equipment.

HOW BREWING USED TO BE DONE

William Cowper wrote a famous book, *Cottage Economy*, bemoaning, amongst other things, the fact that people were being almost forced to stop brewing their own beer, especially in the cities. Most 18th century homes had a copper – a large vessel with a fire under it, in which all the ingredients of beer were boiled, and a series of brewing vessels, from barrels to stoneware pots, to brew in.

The process of fermentation was controlled with lids where the space above the brewing wort became saturated with carbon dioxide, and since oxygen is lighter than carbon dioxide, the right conditions were achieved – so long as the pot wasn't disturbed.

As the 19th century arrived, the majority of people lived in conditions so poor, with no room for brewing in a shared room, the brewing of beer became a commercial proposition. Almost all of our pubs have their origin, one way or another, in that period.

Names of public houses

Actually, the names of public houses in the UK and further afield have interesting origins which, though nothing to do with brewing in itself, is worth a mention.

It was the hope of many sailors and soldiers in Georgian times, to open a public house with the money they earned as bounty. Everything the serviceman did that was of financial value to the country in the course of his duties entitled him to a share of bounty. If they captured a ship, he would get a share of its value, or if they took a town, or took treasure – all these things provided him with cash.

Pubs with names like Gibraltar, Nelson and so on were started by sailors. The Wellington, The Waterloo and so on were started by soldiers.

The public house was just that – a place to go because, particularly in the first half of the 19th century, people lived often in squalid and cramped conditions.

Many public houses brewed their own beer, but slowly through the 19th and early 20th centuries, they were bought out, one by one, by large breweries.

Those public houses sporting the title 'Free House' remained independent, giving themselves the ability to buy beer from breweries if they wanted to, but mostly brewing their own beer on the premises.

This has become replicated in recent days with the advent of the microbrewery, essentially an old-fashioned pub with brewing facilities.

One of the most interesting of pub names is Frog and Bucket, which are the most important tools in the arsenal of any cellerman: the frog to keep the cellar clean, and the bucket for a million beer jobs.

HOW TO MAKE THE BEST BEER IN THE WORLD

First: Take your time

Don't try to rush things. Don't stop the beer brewing when it is not ready. Don't try to warm it up to make it go more quickly. Don't try to drink the beer before it is completely matured.

Second: Be scrupulously clean

Don't try to make a beer or cider in a dirty vessel. They need complete and total cleaning. Wild yeast and bacteria spoil your beer – and can even make it poisonous.

Third: Get to know your ingredients

Experiment and find out how pale malt grains or extract or fluid extract works. How it behaves in certain circumstances. That goes for everything else – how the various hops work, or the numerous different varieties of apple.

MODERN BREWING EXPLAINED

There are a number of ways of brewing beer. The simplest way is to buy a brew kit, of which there are many, and you can brew a variety of beers with great success and get products that taste wonderful. This is usually the route along which most people new to brewing take their first steps, graduating into making beer from raw ingredients, for which you will obviously need more equipment. The following sections will give you a bit more detail about the kind of equipment you might need for the various brewing processes.

Brewing vessels

Brewing vessels are usually plastic and have a large capacity of over 6 gallons, which is around 30 litres. They come in various designs. A simple bucket with a lid is the easiest to use, and certainly the easiest to clean. The lid traps carbon dioxide in the airspace above the brewing liquid. Obviously, the more you remove the lid to see what is going on inside, the more the process is slowed down – but who can resist a quick peek?

Sometimes the lid will have a hole in the centre, to fit a bung with an airlock. If you buy one of this type, be sure that the hole is of standard size, as the last thing you want is to buy bungs of different sizes – they only get lost and you never have the right one when you need it.

Usually, this vessel is used when you plan to bottle your beer.

Pressure vessels

This is a barrel shaped plastic vessel with a tightly screwing lid. Often the lid has no hole in it, which means that pressure will build up in the vessel as the fermentation continues. There is often a tap at the bottom. The idea behind this vessel is as the pressure increases the sediment is forced below the tap. You brew and pour from the same vessel.

You can get another variation of this vessel, with a holed lid for an airlock. This then has looser sediment, but has a wider variety of uses.

Plastic barrel vessels can pose a bit of a problem when it comes to cleaning. Reaching all the surfaces inside is not so easy, and you have to fill them up with water to sterilise all the surfaces. Also, the tap is not that easy to sterilise.

Another problem with taps built into these vessels is that things can crawl up them. I once had the excellent idea of brewing in my greenhouse. After all, it is warm in there – it proved to be a great temperature for brewing! However, having used a pressure vessel, I poured my first pint only to find a slug in my beer. It had crawled up the tap's spout, poor creature, and I nearly drank it.

You can buy little caps for taps; a drawer full will be enough.

Electronic brewing vessels

Jacketed, thermostatically controlled, electric blankets are available for the really serious home brewer. You can set the correct temperature and the fermentation will occur when the brew has reached exactly the right point. These are usually sold with the appropriate vessel, but you can buy them separately.

Mash tun

Brewing from raw materials, grain and so on, frequently needs exact temperatures to soak and rinse the sugars from the grain. The mash tun is a vessel that often has an electric heater, and sometimes a hot water piped system, for keeping the mixture of grains at exactly the right temperature. Sometimes they also come with a sparge system for rinsing and getting as much liquid from the mix.

Needless to say, this sophisticated equipment is not strictly necessary, but a great big stockpot is an absolute must, so you can soak your grains and then sparge with hot water.

There are many kinds of mashing equipment. You can buy really sophisticated (read expensive) equipment which allows you to run almost a mini-microbrewery.

Demijohn

Although these belong more in the realm of the winemaker, you can use these one gallon vessels for brewing apple wine (posh cider) and barley wine. Usually made from glass and with a distinctive shape, in recent years plastic versions of the same vessel have been produced.

Care is needed with demijohns because they are so thin. Boiling water will doubtless end in the cracking of the glass, and if you try to sterilise with heat, disaster will strike. The same goes for the plastic versions which will crumple up with heat. Consequently you can only sterilise them with chemicals.

Another problem is cleaning the inside properly – you need a bottle brush that will reach in the lip.

The demijohn was originally a much larger bottle for home country wine production or for experimenting with recipes, but in its current form has become the mainstay for home wine production.

Airlock

The airlock is simply a twisted tube into which you put a small amount of water. This then allows gasses out of the vessel, but no air in. Some people fit the airlock after a day or so, just so the yeast can reproduce in oxygen solution, fitting it later to encourage fermentation.

You can get many different designs of airlock, fitting all kinds of vessels. In my experience, plastic is much to be preferred to glass.

Fruit millers

These are a series of cogs which break up the fruit, especially apples that have been quartered first. The pulp is then pressed.

Paddle

It is always a good idea to invest in a paddle, even if you are only ever going to do home brewing. It is simply a large spoon with a long handle, and it allows you to get to the very bottom of your brewing vessel without ruining your shirt sleeves trying to do the job with a domestic spoon.

It is one of the quirks of nature that you always dip your sleeve in the brew, and it always ruins your shirt.

Plastic tubing

Becoming a brewer involves a lot of tubing. This is mostly for siphoning fermenting liquid 'off the lees', the lees being a mixture of dead yeast and bits of hops, or cell walls of fruit, etc. Usually this tubing is made of polythene and about 1 cm in diameter. However, people brewing in pressure vessels, or transporting gas to barrels, need to use reinforced tubing, and the appropriate fastener.

Muslin/filtration bags

When mashing all the flavour and sugar from your materials the remaining pulp is caught in a few sheets of muslin, which is finely woven cotton, or a jam bag, which is often made from nylon. Both can be washed, and both need to be sterilised before use. Muslin is cheaper, but less hard-wearing than nylon.

Hydrometer

Every schoolboy knows (well, perhaps in former years . . .) the story of Archimedes having a bath. He suddenly realised the answer to the science behind displacement, got out of the bath, and ran down the street naked shouting 'Eureka!'. Personally, I'm not surprised. What is more surprising is that he wasn't arrested! (Or perhaps he was?)

The point behind displacement is that the object pushed into the water feels an opposing force – it's really Newton's third law, that force is equal to the weight of the liquid displaced.

So when you plonk a hydrometer in the beer, it feels a force which is basically the sum of the force of water, plus whatever is dissolved in it. In our case, more or less, the only difference between unbrewed beer and brewed beer or cider, or wine, is the amount of sugar that has been used in the meantime.

Consequently, there is a direct correlation between the change in sugar concentration and the amount of alcohol replacing it.

Many beer kits call for the use of a hydrometer – though some don't bother. But brewing from raw materials definitely needs one.

Bottles

Right! Confession time. I do not always bottle the brews I create. It isn't always necessary. For example, a demijohn of cider, once racked, might as well stay in the demijohn because there is no real need for it to be bottled – I am going to drink it straight from the bottle, as it were.

PET BOTTLES

Sometimes I use PET lemonade bottles. You can get lemonade for around 17p a bottle at the moment. It isn't worth drinking, but we do keep as much of it as we can in jugs and other containers to keep from wasting it. The main thing about these bottles is they are sterile inside. They make a great container for 2 litres of beer.

Repeating this process means 20 bottles for a full beer kit brew – a lot of lemonade to drink! But there is a good reason to use them beyond their cheapness and sterility. The bottom of the bottle has 4 little lugs in it, into which the sediment falls to make a hard plug that doesn't unravel into the beer as it is poured.

Thankfully, in recent times, these PET bottles have been available specially for home brew in reasonable quantities at a decent price. You can get them in clear or brown plastic and they are ideal for the job. You sterilise them with tablets.

WARNING ABOUT REUSING BOTTLES

Glass bottles are getting thinner and thinner these days, and although it is possible to get hold of and reuse bottles, as we have already said with some lemonade bottles, you are best buying glass ones you know for sure are strong enough to cope with the pressure you are going to exert on them.

Bottle caps

The good old-fashioned metal caps – the sort you need to use a bottle opener for – have, to my mind, always been the best because they are used only once, and they offer the lowest possible chance of spoiling the precious liquid.

Bottle capper

This is a levered machine which puts the caps on the bottles. I must confess that I found it difficult to use at first, because I thought I was going to smash the bottle. But once you get the hang of it, it is easy.

Bottle brush

This is a bendy brush on wire that allows the efficient cleaning of the awkward parts of the bottles, fermentation vessels and even tubes.

Thermometers

I use two thermometers:

- a long glass one, which has easy to read graduations in 1°C. This gives me an accurate reading, which I always try to take before adding yeast;

- a stick-on plastic display thermometer, which I attach to the bucket so I can keep my eye on the general temperature during the brewing process.

Filters

There are loads of filtering systems on the market, from simple pour methods through some kind of paper filter, to expensive filters with mechanical pumps and delivery systems.

Presses

This is the best way to get apple juice. First the apples are milled in order to create a pulp, and then the juice is extracted. This gives a super juice for drinking – but it's even better fermented!

The presses these days are usually on a screw principle. The remaining apple pulp is called a cheese.

The most important ingredient

Do you remember the advert on the television for Mackeson? The old chap was sitting by the fire in his cottage, pouring his glass of stout, slowly and carefully in a way every Englishman would have recognised. When full, with a dark creamy head (though the television was in black and white), he would take a sip and then look at the camera with wet lips and say, 'It looks good, it tastes good, and by golly – it does you good!'

Well, it used to make me sad because he was all alone. The most important ingredient is company, someone to drink with, preferably a crowd.

FINDING OUT THE ALCOHOL CONTENT OF BEER

Finding out the alcohol content of a beer is essentially done by working out where all the sugar went – in other words, you need to find out the specific gravity (SG) of the beer. You might want to come back to this time and again – it took me ages to get it, and I still don't always get it right. The fact is you don't really need to refer to the SG unless you are making a new beer, or following a complex recipe. (This chapter also deals with how to follow a beer recipe, use a hydrometer and how to change and experiment with beers.)

This is a bit technical, but fairly essential if you are going to understand what is going on in your brewing, how much alcohol there is in the final product and how to adjust it if you do not have the right results.

The use of a hydrometer to control your brewing is not difficult, and if you want to go on to create a beer that is reproducible, batch after batch, it is an important step. There is a huge difference in flavour between a beer that is 3.3% alcohol and one that is 4.2%. If the brew is calculated to not ferment out all the sugars in the pot, clearly it will have a different flavour, a maltier flavour, than one that is left until the various sugars are gone.

The fermentation is stopped by adding Campden tablets, when a certain specific gravity is reached.

Specific gravity, as the term suggests, implies weight. If I drop a glass bubble in air it will fall to the ground and smash on the floor. If I drop it in water it will float, but will have fallen a little – displacing an amount of liquid in the process. The weight, or force, of the liquid on the bubble is exactly the weight of the displacement.

I can make the liquid 'stronger' by dissolving something in it – in our case, sugar. The more sugar you add, the higher the bubble will sit on the water.

A hydrometer is simply a glass bubble with lead weights inside, and a thin top from which you read the 'strength' or specific gravity.

Using a hydrometer

As stated above, a hydrometer is a glass bubble which has a long thin tube at one end and a lead weight at the other. In the tube there is usually a piece of paper with graduations that have numbers printed on the side.

Most hydrometers come with a measuring tube that you fill with a sample and insert the hydrometer. To use it:

- Make sure the hydrometer is clean and sterile.

- Let the sample warm up to room temperature before testing and tap away any air bubbles.

- Read the number at the top of the meniscus – this is the specific gravity of the sample.

Amount of sugar

For the most part, the change in specific gravity (as near as makes no difference) depends on the amount of sugar you add. Technically these are known as 'degrees Plato' in beer brewing and 'degrees Brix' in wine making. But then the majority of brewing recipes talk in terms of just plain old specific gravity.

The more sugar you add, the greater the SG or degrees Plato, etc. You can use your hydrometer as scales, as a change in SG reflects the amount of sugar dissolved in the liquid.

Water has an SG of 1.00 which means that 1 litre of water weighs 1 kg. If I add 50 g sugar it would have an SG of 1.05, which means a litre weighs 1050 g.

In the brewing world we use grams as the basic unit, therefore the SG of pure water is 1000, and with 50 g sugar it becomes 1050.

The specific gravity of beer-making worts varies from as low as 1040 for mild beers and session beers to 1080 for barley wines. Of course, wines are much stronger, with a starting gravity of 1090 or more.

Original and final gravity

The calculation of how much alcohol there is in the final product means taking a note of the change in gravity during the brewing process. Essentially, the specific gravity of the liquid is a measure of the density of the material, and as sugar molecules are converted to carbon dioxide and alcohol, the specific gravity will reduce as fermentation continues.

Sometimes recipes will require you to stop the fermentation at a specific gravity. This is done to provide consistent results because, so long as you stick to the recipe, you should have a specified amount of alcohol, and the drink will have a certain sweetness too. There is a lot more to the final flavour than just alcohol content, and the amount of sugar that is allowed to be left in the drink is important – particularly because a lot of the flavour comes from the action of the yeast.

Calculating alcohol content

There are lots of different formulations for working out the actual alcohol content, but the simplest, one that gives you a fairly accurate measure, is original gravity minus final gravity, multiplied by 131.

So, for example:

Original gravity 1050
Final gravity 1025

The difference is 25, multiplied by 131 = 3.275%
The online alcohol calculator made it 3.3% – a great mild session beer.

TEMPERATURE CONSIDERATIONS

In theory at least, the standard temperature for testing specific gravity is 60°F, and in order to get a really accurate reading the liquids need to be at this temperature. However, should you just let the samples attain room temperature, this should be good enough, besides, who is going to quibble about a couple of tenths of a percentage point?

BEER RECIPES AND HOW TO FOLLOW THEM

On the whole in this book you will encounter recipes in a cooking format. That is, the recipe tells you to do this and that at specific times, using a number of methods. On the internet, however, there are thousands of recipes for home brewing, and they don't all make sense at first inspection.

Let's have a look at a beer recipe, exactly as you would find it on the internet, and go through it in some detail. You can then plunge deeply into the world of beer!

Type: Extract	*Date: 6/25/2003*
Boil Size: 10.00 gal	*Brewer: Rob Dryman*
Boil Time: 60 min	*Equipment: Brick House Brewery*
Taste Rating (out of 50): 35.0	*Brewhouse Efficiency:*
Taste Notes: A great American amber Ale that is similar to the great microbrew found in the Pacific northwest.	

Ingredients

16.00 lb Pale Liquid Extract (8.0 SRM) Extract 91.17%

1.25 lb Caramel/Crystal Malt – 40 L (40.0 SRM) Grain 7.12%

0.15 lb Peat Smoked Malt (2.8 SRM) Grain 0.85%

0.15 lb Roasted Barley (300.0 SRM) Grain 0.85%

1.00 oz Northern Brewer [8.50%] (60 min) Hops 15.2 IBU

0.50 oz Cascade [5.50%] (60 min) Hops 4.4 IBU

0.50 oz Northern Brewer [8.50%] (15 min) Hops 3.8 IBU

0.50 oz Cascade [5.50%] (15 min) Hops 2.2 IBU

0.50 oz Northern Brewer [8.50%] (5 min) Hops 1.5 IBU

0.50 oz Cascade [5.50%] (5 min) Hops 0.9 IBU

1 Pkg Burton Ale (White Labs #WLP023) Yeast-Ale

Beer Profile

Original Gravity: 1.058 SG

Final Gravity: 1.016 SG

Estimated Alcohol by Vol: 5.55%	
Bitterness: 28.0 IBU	*Calories: 43 cal/pint*
Est Color: 12.6 SRM	*Color: Color*
Mash Profile	
Mash Name: None	*Total Grain Weight: 10.00 lb*
Sparge Water:	*Grain Temperature:*
Sparge Temperature:	*Tun Temperature:*
Adjust Temp for Equipment: FALSE	*Mash PH:*
Steep grains as desired (30–60 minutes)	
Mash Notes:	
Carbonation and Storage	
Carbonation Type: Corn Sugar	*Volumes of CO_2: 2.4*
Pressure/Weight:	*Carbonation Used:*
Keg/Bottling Temperature: 60.0°F	*Age for: 28 days*
Storage Temperature: 52.0°F	
Notes	
Steep the grains in 4 gallons of water at 150°F for 30 minutes. Bring to boil and add the extract, boil according to schedule.	

There are many more recipes like this out there on the internet. I counted 2,765 recipes for different beers on the web, and I am sure there are lots more, each with interesting names.

You would have thought each recipe would give you everything you need to actually brew the beer, but they often don't provide a method or distinct instructions – you have to make decisions yourself.

However, having gone through a couple of recipes, you will find it fairly easy to work out what to do. Notice that this recipe came from an American website, and consequently you will have to adjust all the various measurements.

Although the recipe doesn't give you everything, as we said, you can still take it as a guide for making your own beer. Let's look at the information in the recipe in a bit more detail, taking each heading in turn:

Type: Extract
This is an extract rather than a whole grain or malted grain recipe. This tells you that at some point the extract will be boiled, but if you read the recipe carefully you will see that you have to steep some grains too. Using grain and extract together is very common in these recipes.

Boil size
This is the amount of liquid you are going to boil with the extract.

Boil time
This is the length of time you are going to boil the extract.

Ingredients
There are a lot of ingredients in this beer, possibly too many. The majority of the content of the brew, or the 'bill' as it is sometimes called, is pale malt extract. This beer is more or less a pale ale – but you don't have to tell the Americans.

SRM

You will notice a number of references to SRM in the recipe. This is the Standard Reference Method of determining colour. I have to confess, for my brewing, I prefer to make beer that is sort of the right colour. Besides, I can never get the hang of looking at the colour of the beer when the glass is actually at my mouth.

Besides, if you were going to the shop to buy these ingredients, you would have difficulty finding caramel/crystal malt (40.0 SRM). In most of the shops you will find you will have to make do with plain old crystal malt.

So in following recipes you are really making decisions about what will fit the bill.

Original gravity/final gravity

These refer to the initial sugar content and how much of this is used up in the brewing, as described earlier.

Bitterness

In the recipe you will see a figure, 28 IBU, which shows you two things. First, it shows that this is an American recipe – if it were European, it would have EBU. Secondly, and more importantly, this is a measure of bitterness, and goes from a scale of 0 (not bitter) to 120 (very bitter indeed).

The bitterness is achieved by adding certain hops and there is no point in thinking of measuring it yourself. The IBU (EBU) is often printed on packets of various hops and so on.

Mash profile

There isn't much detail in this recipe here, which tells you everything is pretty standard. The mash temperature is around 65°C. The sparge temperature is similar and the pH is not important. There is a note that says, 'steep grains as desired, 30–60 minutes', which means you can steep them for 90 minutes if you like, though I would stick to an hour in this case.

Carbonation and storage

The most important thing here is that it says the carbonation method is corn sugar. There are two ways of doing this. Firstly you can add 50 g corn sugar to the keg (dissolved in a little water) and this will bring about secondary fermentation to put more carbon dioxide in the brew. Secondly, you can add a teaspoon to each bottle when you decant the beer and seal it.

Notes

This is possibly the most important part of the whole recipe. Here you get a hint of how to make the beer – sometimes!

VARIATIONS IN RECIPES

Don't forget, there are thousands of recipes out there, and you sometimes have to take them with a pinch of salt. But they are a great starting point for your own beer experimenting.

There are three essential ways of experimenting with beers to make your own: changing the sugar content; changing the yeast; or adding something.

Changing the sugar content

This is done in many ways – for example, you can change malt grains to malt extract. All the different types of malt, that we will see in later chapters, pale malt, amber malt, brown malt, chocolate malt (each going darker as you go along) have a grain and an extract equivalent form.

As a rule, grains are steeped (or mashed) at about 66°C to allow the enzymes in the seeds to convert the starch to sugars. Then the liquid is washed into a pan and brought to the boil. The beer flavours develop as you boil, so often the boiling can be more than an hour in length.

Extract malts are merely boiled, as all the sugars are extracted for you. Again, the flavours are developed as they boil.

You might – as you will see in the instructions for making kit beer (see Chapter 3) – replace sugar with pale malt extract, which is very easy and always gives an excellent beer.

Similarly, you might want to swap some of the malt or sugar with honey. You will need to remember that honey is only 80% sugar, so account for this in your calculations.

Changing the yeast

This is an important step to take as a lot of the flavour comes from the type of yeast. As a general rule, ciders are brewed with wine yeast and beer with various beer yeasts. You can experiment with them, but generally the ale yeasts are for dark beer, ordinary beer yeasts are for pale ale, etc., and the German yeasts are for lager.

Adding something

We have recipes for Christmas beer with mullings (spices) and a beer kit with nettle juice in it. You can brew beers with fruit juice and all kinds of additives.

Be careful – don't add too many, and you do need to think about clashing flavours as you go. It is (or should be) a crime to pour beer away, and 22.5 litres is a lot to have to drink if you don't like it.

Simple changes are easy – like turning a pale ale recipe to a mild beer recipe by substituting chocolate malt for some of the pale malt – so go ahead and mess about. Playing with beer is a lot more interesting than playing computer games – so get on with it!

STERILISING YOUR EQUIPMENT

It is vastly important that you sterilise your equipment before brewing. Not just so that you know it is clean, but so that it is biologically clean.

Fermentation works on the principle that an organism gets energy, and thus reproduces itself (which seems to be the only goal in the life of a yeast) from sugar. How many millions of other organisms do the same?

A small army of microbes are ready to invade your brew, and many of them can be quite troublesome. If you can imagine a heaven for microbes, it would be warm, wet and loaded with sugar. Can beer or cider be any more wonderful a place for a microbe to live?

Microbes breed quickly

Bacteria will divide every 20 minutes, so a single bacterium – *E. coli* is a good example – will double in number each 20-minute period, making 1.2 million bacteria at the end of day one.

However, there are some parts of your beer that fight this growth, especially hops and the increasing alcohol content.

However, you can imagine the importance of making sure nothing can get into your brew other than your ingredients. Consequently it is important to make sure everything is completely sterilised.

Wash everything first

It isn't easy to disinfect any vessels if they have various amounts of debris on them from previous brewing. Try to get into the habit of cleaning them out as soon as you have done with them so it is easier to wash them through at a later date.

You will need a good bottle brush to reach all those difficult places, and I use a toilet brush, kept for the purpose of course, to help me scrub at the inside of beer kegs.

Using chloride based sterilisers

Fundamentally, this is bleach – and various concentrations of bleach can be used to clean various vessels and implements. Chlorine based cleaners come in various forms. Tablets, which you simply dissolve in water, are the most convenient – a demijohn is easily cleaned with a couple of tablets.

You can also buy the same material in liquid form, where usually a capful in a gallon of water does the job.

Using Campden tablets or sulphite

You can use these for disinfecting – though they are not as commonplace as chlorine-based tablets and are therefore harder to come by, and possibly more expensive. They are very useful – indispensible in fact – for killing yeast and stopping the fermentation process.

No boil

Years ago it was simple. Earthenware containers were boiled to make sure they were clean inside, as were wooden barrels. Today the majority of home brewers have to put up with flimsy materials. Most brewing equipment will not cope with boiling. Demijohns are usually so thin they will crack if heated to temperatures higher than 40°C and the plastic ones crumple when in contact with boiling water.

The same goes for fermentation vessels of all kinds. Besides, they are usually too large to fill with boiling water anyway.

Cleaning large vessels

This is the trickiest cleaning job, but before you start to sterilise, make sure it is all spotlessly clean in the first place. Use detergent and scrub away the leftovers, if there are any.

The dilution effect

Rinsing with tap water is fine, but when you have done that, rinse again with cool boiled water to dilute and remove anything left behind by the rinsing water.

Then disinfect

The simple way to disinfect is to fill the vessel with cold water and add the appropriate amount of cleaning tablets/powder/liquid. You can also submerge all your other utensils, airlock, paddles for stirring, bowls, lids and tubes for racking in the vessel and sterilise the lot in one go.

Sometimes this is not convenient and the large vessel has to be disinfected with a stronger solution. A cupful of bleach allowed to work on all the sides and bottom of a vessel is enough to disinfect it.

TAKE CARE: YOU MUST USE PROTECTIVE CLOTHING, PROTECTIVE GLASSES AND GLOVES, AND DO NOT BREATHE THE FUMES.

Then rinse everything as thoroughly as you can.

Cleaning tubing

When cleaning a 22.5 litre vessel, instead of just pouring the liquid away, siphon it first through the tube you are going to use for racking. To do this, fill the tube with cold water and use this as the siphon starter to drag the sterilising solution through into the drain.

This takes about 20 minutes to empty the vessel – time enough to sterilise the inside of the tube.

Cleaning utensils

Anything that is tube based, like an airlock, needs to have a constant change of cleaning solution, so every few minutes, shake it empty and then refill it again with fresh solution from your batch.

Wooden and rubber materials, paddles, bungs, towels can be boiled before use and then cleaned immediately. It is a good idea, when using implements during the brewing process, to have a towel set aside specially for the purpose. Take a little cleaning solution and soak the towel in it. Then fold carefully and place it on a tray.

When you are not using the implement, put it in the fold of the towel. Give the towel a good rinse before you put it to be washed.

No peering

When you are actually making your brew, don't keep on peering in the bucket, don't have big sniffs of beer aroma, and where possible leave the lid in place while you do other things. If you need to inspect the brew, then just lift the lid partially, and for as short a time as possible.

Storage

Keep brewing material separate from any other implements in the house. For example, it is possible to use siphons for almost any liquid, but you will taint your beer if you use the same piece of tube for multiple uses. Try to keep a separate pan for boiling grains and malt than the one you use for making jam. Don't use the same funnels and keep sugars separate.

It is a good idea to have a brewing cupboard rather than rummaging around the kitchen for bits and pieces.

New equipment

It should be obvious that new glassware, equipment, utensils and so on are not sterile and will need a good cleaning and sterilising just the same as any other piece of equipment.

Sterilising beer bottles

Brewers' houses are frequently stuffed to the rafters with beer bottles of all shapes and sizes, and there are two basic ways of sterilising them before use: with heat, or with bleach. For either method it goes without saying that you will have washed the bottles inside first, and rinsed them a number of times to remove any aroma either of beer or of detergent.

USING HEAT

If you have a pasteuriser, or a large pan, you can fill the pan to the halfway point with water and stand the bottles upright in it before placing the lid on and bringing it to the boil. Keep a rolling boil going for 15 minutes and then use tongs to pull the bottles out. Be very careful at this point – the bottles will be very hot and the hot water itself is dangerous.

Tip out any liquid that might have wandered in and stand the bottles upright to cool. A small piece of aluminium foil over the tops keeps the inside safe.

USING BLEACH

Bring a pan of water to the boil and immerse your bottles in the boiling liquid, making sure there are no air bubbles in the bottles. Again, be careful. Add the appropriate amount of bleach (or tablets as described above) to the water and allow the liquid to cool.

By the time the water is cool – everything inside will be sterile.

BOTTLING YOUR BEER

This is the way beer is presented and stored. Beer, once bottled, is not actually finished at all. It is in fact still undergoing changes, as complex sugars are being made, large molecules are breaking down and the substance in the bottle is maturing.

Secondary fermentation

The primary and main fermentation has taken place in the fermenting bin and the beer is fizzy because carbon dioxide is dissolved in the water. However, the bottling process can reduce this, and some maturation is frequently needed too. A small amount of sugar – a teaspoon per bottle – is added to the bottle to encourage a secondary fermentation, and therefore an amount of gas is dissolved in the beer in the bottle.

This creates a little sediment in the bottom of the bottle too – which means you have to pour the beer carefully.

To avoid this, some recipes add sugar, dissolved in hot water, to the racked beer before bottling. Half a cup of corn sugar in a cup of water is the usual dose to gas up the beer.

Sterilise

Obviously, everything needs to be sterilised before bottling, including your siphon and lids.

Cool your bottles and take your time

In all bottling, do it slowly. The last thing you want to do is waste a load of beer by forming a huge head in the bottle, and not have the ability to get it down. Pour the beer in slowly on to the side of the bottle. If you put your bottles in the freezer first, this will lessen the tendency of the beer to create a head when bottling. Always slide the beer down the side of the glass and maintain a constant trickle until the bottle is full to within 3 cm of the top.

Using a funnel and a siphon

You need plenty of room to work and be sure you have siphon-ability (what I mean is make sure your bottles are well below the level of the liquid).

Place a funnel in the neck of your bottle and then use the siphon to fill it. The siphon should be a soft plastic tube so you can stop the flow by squeezing the tube – not by placing your thumb over the end.

If you are adding sugar at the bottling stage, put it into the funnel before you fill, and wash it down with the siphoned beer.

Using a keg with a tap

The tendency in this case is simply to leave the beer in the keg, but I prefer to bottle from a keg because it is easy. Charge the secondary fermentation in the keg rather than in the bottle and wait a few days for it to ferment out.

Simply put the bottle under the tap and pour from the keg.

Using a capping machine

You can buy caps from the brew shop, and the capping machine then places them neatly on the top of the bottle. Always buy the correct caps for the appropriate bottles. Don't try to fill wine bottles with fizzy beer, they are likely to smash – always buy appropriate bottles.

The capper works on a lever system to crimp the caps in place. If you can afford it, a bench capper is a much better buy than a double-handed lever-type capper. The bench capper is much easier to use, the bottles are held in place more easily and the success rate is 99.9999%. You cannot always say that for a double-handed one.

Storing the bottles

Unlike wine, beer in bottles is stored standing upright, and should be in a cool, dark place – not in a fridge and definitely not in the freezer.

Don't forget the label

The label is important. You want to know – because you will forget – exactly what the beer is, what went into it and when you made it. The label can be pretty if you like, but make sure all you need to know is on it.

CHAPTER 2

UNDERSTANDING WHAT GOES INTO A PINT OF BEER

There are so many words bandied about in the brewing world, especially when using raw materials, it makes your head spin (even more than the beer does).

So, in this chapter we will just take a quick overall look at what materials go into a pint, and then, just to prove the whole process is just as easy as a kit beer, we'll go through the process of making a simple beer at the end of the chapter.

When you look at recipes for home brewing from scratch, it is easy to get confused because there are so many differently-named ingredients. Although this can be quite bewildering, the names are basically there to correlate with the type of beer you are going to produce.

THE BASIC FUNDAMENTALS EXPLAINED

It takes seven minutes for a burst of energy to leave the sun and travel through the solar system for 93 million miles. Its journey's end is to crash into a specially modified, microscopic organelle in a leaf of the grass we know as barley. Its energy is released and the plant cleverly uses it to make sugar, some of which ends up in a seed, where it is made insoluble, individual molecules being stacked together to make starch.

There it stays, until the seed is wetted. An enzyme in the seed converts this starch into sugar, ready to give off its energy to give life to the seed. This in itself is pure miracle, with more to come. When the enzyme completes its work converting starch, it is released back into the wort to convert even more starch.

Malt and wort

If you take a load of barley seeds and wet them, then leave them in a warm room, they just begin to sprout. The process is then stopped, i.e. the just-sprouting grains are killed, by increasing the temperature, and then it is roasted in a kiln until it reaches a specified colour. The malted barley is then taken away and cured so it can sit on the shelf for some time, before you buy it and mash it. Barley that has been treated in this way is called malted barley, and is referred to as malt.

The enzyme in the seed is quite robust, and whereas most proteins are denatured, or broken up, at temperatures above 40°C, this particular one will tolerate higher temperatures.

What we have now is barley seeds with some sugar, some starch and some enzymes (amylase) in them. Mashing is the process of dissolving the sugars from the malt. So, if you put the malt in a pan and soak it at a temperature of around 65°C for an hour or so, the remaining enzymes will get to work converting all the starch into sugar, so what you have is a sugary liquid called wort. This is what you brew!

UNDERSTANDING THE DIFFERENCE BETWEEN BASE AND NON-BASE MALTS

A base malt has lots of enzymes to convert the rest of the starch into sugar. Unless you are using neat sugar in your brew, you need to add base malt as a fundamental starting point. Other malts, such as chocolate malt, make use of the enzymes in your base malt to remove any sugars.

Other malts are often added to achieve certain colours and so on.

But it's not as simple as that

When you go into your home-brew shop you can be put off by the number of malts there are to choose from, as well as some of the other seemingly silly names.

The colours of malt depend mostly on how long they have been roasted, and are measured in Lovibond rating, after a system devised in the 1880s by a Mr J W Lovibond, strangely enough.

Crystal malt

This is the exception to the rule because it is not kilned. It is stewed at about 60°C so that the enzymes get to work converting all the starch to sugar. It is then prepared for the shelf. As it dries the sugar crystallises to give hard pieces of sugar. Consequently it is called crystal malt.

It is also known in some places as caramel malt.

Because it is almost pure sugar, you don't need to mash it – it is simply crushed and boiled in water, so you have the extracted sugars in the wort. It also provides some colour to the beer.

Spray malt

If you spray dry malted grains you get a completely soluble, sugar-rich malt powder, that has maltiness about it, but can be used instead of sugar in beer kits, or in simple beer production.

If you want to enhance a beer kit, use spray malt instead of sugar.

Pale malt

This is possibly one of the most important malts on the market. It is used not only for pale ale but bitter beers and a number of others. It is also the starting point for many designer beers.

It is basically cheap malty sugar for mashing.

Amber malt

This is darker than pale malt and is toasted. It is used in the production of porter and some brown ales. You can make your own amber malt by toasting pale malt on a baking tray in the oven until it has reached the colour you want.

Brown malt

This is even darker still than amber malt – it is roasted for longer, and is used in brown ale production. This malt has no enzymes in it, and is often mashed with other malts to help get to all the sugar.

Chocolate malt

This is roasted until dark brown, and some of the sugars are caramelised to give a unique flavour. It is used to make best mild beers, some dark stouts and porters.

Black malt

This is roasted until it is black, and is used to make porter and dark stout. It is also used to bring up the colour of some beers, a handful being enough.

Pilsner malt

This is a German invention used to create lager. It comes from the lightest malt – hardly roasted much at all, and if you have picked up the trend, the lighter the malt the more enzymes there are in it (because it is not over-heated) and therefore you can use Pilsner malt as a base malt.

Pilsner malt is quite strongly flavoured and can be used to make a multitude of beers. Sometimes you get carapils malt in the UK, which is a similar product.

Other malts

There are a number of malts on the market that are rarely, if ever, used by home brewers. Vienna malt, Munich malt, acid malt and so on, have their characteristic roles to play – usually in brewing European beers.

USING WHOLE GRAINS

Often non-malted grains are used in brewing. Using whole grains is an important step in the production of brown ale.

Roasted barley

This is barley, un-malted, but roasted until it is dark brown. It is added to a base malt and produces a dark stout.

Flaked barley

Flaked barley looks a little like cornflakes. It is made from barley which is roasted until it is dark, and is used in stout and Guinness.

Torrified wheat

If you like a good head, one that lasts to the bottom of the glass, a handful of torrified wheat in the brew is sufficient. Torrified means 'puffed up' and is easy to use – just throw a handful in.

USING HOPS

Hops are used to flavour and preserve beer. They have a bitter flavour and produce chemicals that stop spoilage by oxidation. There are lots of varieties of hops which give their own distinctive taste to the beer, and they are often used in combination with others.

Here are just a few you will find on the shelves:

Admiral
This is really citrus in flavour and is used as a bitter for pale ale and best bitter. It is quite strong, but really refreshing. A lot of microbreweries use this variety for bottled beers.

Cascade
This is an American hop that is available worldwide. It has very strong flavours and is resistant to fungal infections, so is easy to grow. It makes a good hoppy beer.

Fuggles
One of the oldest of hops, this has quite a bitter punch to it, and can be harsh.

Northern Brewer
This is a 20th century multi-purpose hop. It has a warmth to it, not overpowering, and is a good substitute for a lot of other hops. Classically it can be combined 50:50 with hops like Goldings and Fuggles.

Goldings
There are lots of varieties of Goldings, mainly from Kent, including East Kent, Kent, and just Goldings, amongst others. They are all interchangeable in one way or another, but all have great flavour – brilliant in both bitter and pale ale.

Northdown
A modern hop, comparatively speaking, with a mild hop flavour. This one is great for mild beer.

Phoenix
No, it isn't grown on ashes, but this is another new hop with a mild, if slightly spicy flavour. It is great for bitter when mixed with Goldings.

Target
This is a Fuggles-type hop with a reasonable flavour – good for mild beer.

How do hops preserve the beer?

When you read about hops in recipes, especially on the web, you will notice some discussion of alpha acid content. Alpha acids are a series of very complex acids found in resin glands in flowers. They are what give the hops their flavour.

Alpha acids are a group of compounds which have a number of different flavours – often bitterness. Humulones, a complex group of ketones, are mostly what give the hops their bitterness. There are a number of different humulones, which are chemically quite complex, and different hops have different amounts and proportions. The brewing industry makes sure they have exactly the same flavour from brew to brew. Luckily we amateurs can revel in the differences between brews.

Also, the drying of hops reduces the amounts of alpha acids, as does the age of the hops. Before buying hops, have a check how they have been stored: Are they near the radiator? Are they loose and open to evaporation?

Get the freshest you can, preferably vacuum sealed.

Hops preserve beer only a little. Alcohol, and other substances in the brew, does the rest. The addition of hops does not mean you can be more slapdash with your cleanliness technique.

Hops do, however, have a very definite anti bacterial effect. The humulone and its derivatives kill some bacteria outright and stop others from reproducing.

PUTTING IT ALL TOGETHER: MAKING YOUR BEER

The best way to put things into practice is to make a beer.

Simple bitter

This is a good quality drink, easily produced, and is kind to the brewer, coping well with variations (such as a heavy hand with the ingredients!).

The reason for putting this recipe here is to show you how easy it is to brew your own beer from more or less raw materials. Actually it is hardly any different from using a kit.

Ingredients
To make 22.5 litres:

> 3 kg pale malt extract
> 750 g brewing sugar
> 125 g crystal malt
> 125 g Goldings hops
> Top fermenting beer yeast

Have ready a sterile fermentation vessel, muslin bag and airlock

Method
- Be sure everything is sterilised and perfectly clean for use.
- Boil the pale malt extract and the crystal malt, and half the hops, in 4 litres of water for 15 minutes.
- Strain the wort into a fermentation vessel and pour boiling water over the leftover hops to get the last dregs of sugar and flavour out. This is called sparging. The sparging water goes into your vessel with your wort.

- Stir in the sugar.
- Put the remaining hops in a muslin bag and add to the brew.
- Make up to 22.5 litres with cold water.
- Check the temperature is within the region of 18–21°C.
- Sprinkle top acting yeast on the surface and put on the lid. Set the airlock in place if necessary.
- It should take about 14 to 21 days to ferment. Look inside from time to time to remove excess scum, which has bitter flavours.
- When stopped, you should remove the hops bag and rack off the lees.
- If the beer doesn't clear, you can use finings or you can simply stand it on a stone floor – the solidity of the stone floor gives the brew stability, and minimises the chances of disturbing it; if you put it on a wooden floor, the vibrations do affect the brew.
- Rack into a keg if you wish, or bottle (following the instructions on page 44).

This really is a great beer – simple, but very palatable, taking about a further three weeks to mature.

MAKING FUN BEER

There are loads of fun beers around the place. These include the whacky and often awesome beers that are just out of the ordinary, left field. They are an example of what you can do when you want to be creative in a beery way.

Some of these beers are sold all over the world, and are particularly enjoyed in Belgium and Holland.

Chilli beer

The growing of chillies, making chilli jam and all kinds of curries and the stuff with carne, has become a male bastion these days. The chilli has taken over the BBQ as the accessory of choice for a bloke. So it comes as no surprise to find chilli beer! Only don't get hiccups, and watch out – some of those chillies burn on the way in, and burn on the way out!

(Make this at your own peril! The management accept no liability for burned bottoms, shrivelled tongues or 'orrible oesophaguses!)

Ingredients
To make 4.5 litres:

    500 g barley grains
    500 g raisins
    15 g hot chillies
    1.5 kg brewing sugar
    Teaspoon of beer yeast

Have ready a sterile fermentation vessel, demijohn, bung and airlock – and some gloves

Method
- Chop the chillies and remove the seeds (wear gloves for this part!), and chop up the raisins. Mix in the barley grains.
- Place the mix in a pan and pour over 3 litres of boiling water. Leave to stand for 24 hours.
- Add the liquid to a clean fermenting vessel and make up to 5 litres with boiling water.
- Add the rest of the ingredients except the yeast and stir well.
- After three days of regular stirring, strain into a demijohn and add the yeast, fit an airlock and ferment to completion.

- Add a Campden tablet when the bubbles stop and then rack into a clean demijohn. I keep this for a couple of months and pour from the demijohn rather than bottling it.

This has a hot bite, and is very similar to the barley wine recipe in the strong ale chapter (see page 101).

Kriek beer

This is bottled and sold over most of Europe. Flavoured with cherries, this beer is easy to make, as you simply take a basic lager recipe and add cherries to it.

Ingredients
To make 22.5 litres:

2 kg pale malt extract
500 g brewing sugar
1 kg stoned cherries
75 g Saaz hops
Lager yeast

Have ready a sterile fermentation vessel and airlock

Method
- You need fresh cherries for this, which you have to crush hard to remove the juice. I bring them to the boil in a litre of water, and then decant the liquor into the wort. Then put them in a press to drive out the last dregs of juice.
- Dissolve the hops and the malt in 4.5 litres of water and add the sugar when you bring the lot to the boil. Boil for 30 minutes.
- Strain the liquid off into your fermenting vessel and then sparge the solids with a kettle of hot water.

- Make up to 22.5 litres. Check the temperature and if between 18–21°C, pitch the yeast.
- Leave to grow in aerated water for three days then add the airlock.
- Leave to brew out and then rack off into a second vessel, keeping in the garage or some other cool place for a month.
- Bottle in the normal way (see instructions on page 44).

This is a really smooth drink – it's a cherry version of lager and lime, but the cherry flavour is changed because of the brewing – one could otherwise just add cherry juice!

How to mull beer

For hundreds of years this was the way to drink beer. It was often finished off by putting a hot poker into the beer too.

Ingredients

Per pint of beer you need to add:

1 pinch ground ginger
1 pinch ground nutmeg
2 cm cinnamon stick
2 cloves – slightly crushed
A tablespoon of honey

Method

- Warm the beer in a pan and stir in all the ingredients. You could bring it to the boil, by which time the beer would be fairly low in alcohol.

CHAPTER 3

HOW TO MAKE BEER FROM A KIT

If this is your first attempt at brewing your own beer, you probably feel tentative, a little scared. You're probably wondering if brewing at home is the result of some sort of secret knowledge, and whether you can really do it or not.

FIND YOURSELF A GOOD BREW SHOP

Perhaps the most important thing you can do right now, is to find a good brew shop. Sure, there are many supermarkets and stores where you can buy this equipment, but you are far less likely to get the encouragement and information you need.

My local shop is run by a really cheery chap called Steve, and his shop is called Spitting Feathers. It is crammed from floor to ceiling with beer kits, brew buckets, siphons, wine kits – everything you could imagine for brewing. But it wouldn't be so brilliant a place to buy from if it wasn't for Steve himself, who is not only really knowledgeable about beer, but is just a nice guy to talk to. Your local beer shop will become a valuable resource for knowledge as well as kit, and you will probably get loads of free stuff too.

I know from experience the idea that if you buy anonymously from a supermarket, no one is going to try to sell you something you do not need, but (and I can't talk for every shop in the country) a brew shop makes its living from you coming back and buying again and again. So be sure to visit Steve, or the myriad of other Steves around the country selling beer equipment in the confidence that you will come home with just the right equipment at just the right price.

STERILISING YOUR EQUIPMENT

When you are using a brew kit, possibly the most important thing is to be spotlessly and ruthlessly clean, sterilising everything you are going to use and making the area where you are working sterile too.

The reason for this is that the modern brew kit is diluted with fresh water from the tap. Although you use hot water to get the wort out of the tin, it is then topped up to the five gallon mark with cold water, and this is all but guaranteed to contain some microbes. You can reduce some of the load by filtering the water using one of those filtered purifiers.

Don't be tempted to boil your equipment to sterilise it. The probability is that you have plastic equipment – boiling is too harsh for the plastic and it will misshape. Instead, use either Campden tablets, which release sulphur dioxide to sterilise, or one of the numerous tablets available for sterilising babies' bottles, which release chlorine.

I tend to soak all the smaller items in a bowl of the correct strength sterilising solution, and then half fill the fermentation vessel with the lid on. I make a stronger solution than I need for this, soak the bottom half and then turn it over to do the other half.

Of course, if you are using steel containers, which you may well go on to do at some point, you can boil them clean.

Other sterilisers

Having used your kit once, you will have to clean away all the debris. It is best to do this straight away because the yeast, once dried in, is really difficult to shift. You can buy combined cleaners and sterilisers that help remove the debris as well as the germs.

Once you have had a go, you will probably resort, like most people, to using bleach on the vessels, washed away with cooled, boiled water. It gives you the confidence that everything is clear.

THE CONTENTS OF THE BREW KIT

Quite literally, most beer kits contain no preservatives or nasty chemicals, just beer juice – the wort, which comes in a can. The kit includes a sachet of yeast nutrient, normally vitamin C and some other substances. Similarly, it sometimes includes a packet of finings for clearing, but this is often only supplied with wine and some ciders. Finally, your brew kit will contain a packet of yeast.

Yeast

Don't be tempted to use your own yeast if you have brewed before. The kit has the right yeast for the job and should you substitute another it will severely alter the final flavour.

WHY IS THE RIGHT YEAST IMPORTANT?

Actually, it is the chemistry of the yeast that imparts much of the flavour to the final product. It is at least 50% ingredients and 50% yeast that creates the delicate flavours of beer and cider.

Once I tried an experiment to test this and made a batch of wine using fast action bread yeast. The final drink tasted of bread! I suppose I shouldn't be surprised. If you make a brew using only a syrup solution of sugar and water, the final result does have some flavour, imparted by the yeast you use. We used to do an experiment in the good old days of school science where some syrup was fermented for only a few minutes, and the alcohol removed by distillation. There was a very yeasty aroma that clung for weeks and made you want to nip out for a pint at lunchtime.

WHY DOES YEAST STOP WORKING?

As the fermentation continues, yeasts decrease in efficiency because they are being poisoned by the concentration of alcohol. There is an optimum alcoholic level for the specific yeasts, and this is reflected in the usual strength of beers, ciders and wines. The temperature also has an important role to play. Brewing too warm can cause the yeast to produce spurious alcohols that are not wanted in the brew.

The golden rule with yeast and brew kits is **'don't try to be clever and change things'**.

Campden tablets

Some kits contain Campden tablets. These are sodium metabisulphite, which gives off sulphur dioxide. This has the effect not only of sterilisation, but of killing the yeast, thus stopping fermentation.

MAKING BEER FROM YOUR BREW KIT

Diluting the wort

This is a simple process, and all you need is some boiling water. Actually, you also need protective gloves – the can gets hot! Usually the instructions are in the lid of the kit, or they are printed on the reverse of the wrap-around paper. Read the instructions carefully because they refer to that particular kit, even if you become an expert at brewing from kits.

The wort is all important, and will fall out of the can creating interesting shapes on the way. Use hot water to get the very last dregs of the liquid out of the can, leaving none behind.

The hot water will be cooled later by the addition of cold from the tap, giving you a final temperature around 18–21°C, perfect for brewing.

Adding the sugar

We have already discussed the sucrose/glucose solution. Brewing sugar should always be glucose – particularly for beer and cider. However, some kits require you to add sugar in other forms, often a combination of two sugars.

Usually you need to add 1 kg of sugar to a 22.5 litre/five gallon kit. This might be in the form of a dry malt extract, so to get the best results, read the instructions and buy the correct sugar. Some kits call for only 800 g of sugar – rarely do they call for more than a kilo.

Sugar is sprinkled into the liquid after the wort is diluted, and then the whole lot is stirred with a paddle. It is best to buy a paddle because it reaches down to the bottom of the vessel, giving great 'mixability'. A long spoon or paddle is also easy to clean and sterilise.

There is a correlation between sugar and alcohol production, but you should avoid the temptation to put extra sugar in the brew. It doesn't always increase the amount of alcohol and it usually spoils the balance of the drink.

Topping up with cold water

The action of pouring in jug after jug of water mixes the wort really well. If you can purify the water by filtration, all the better. During this stage, should you have it, add your yeast nutrient. Don't worry if your kit doesn't have yeast nutrient, it may well already be included in the yeast or the wort.

Keeping it at the right temperature

Once your fermentation vessel is full, test the temperature of your brew with a glass thermometer – it should be around 18°C. If not, stand it by a radiator until it reaches this temperature. Don't be tempted to stir the liquid with the thermometer.

Place a plastic colour-change thermometer – the kind you get on fish tanks – on the outside of the vessel so you can keep an eye on the temperature. Keep it as near to 20°C as you can.

Pitching

This is the term given to the way that you sprinkle the yeast on to the surface of the wort. Don't stir it or otherwise mix it. Some yeasts act at the surface, some at the bottom. Rest assured, the yeast will grow as it needs to.

Fitting the seal and airlock

If your system has an airlock, fit it and make sure it is charged with water. I tend to use some of the dilute sterilising liquid, just to be sure nothing grows in there.

The yeast will start to produce carbon dioxide straight away, which at first will be dissolved in the water portion of the wort. The yeast will not be producing alcohol until the oxygen dissolved in the water is running low.

Your brew will take a while to actually start bubbling. With 5 gallons of water it can take a few days for the carbon dioxide to reach saturation level.

Where to put your brewing vessel

Any room is good, but there are a number of provisos. The room should not be a busy one if you can manage it. Lots of vibration unsettles the sediment, and there is also the chance of it being knocked over. I always have some kind of catch system – especially if I am using a small vessel like a demijohn. Sometimes the wort will froth a lot and spill out of the vessel. I can speak with experience about the earache you get when your brewing spoils a wonderful table!

It is an established fact that people who brew on stone floors make better wines and beers than people who have to put their brewing vessels on floorboards. The vibrations of a whole house mix the sediment but stone floors offer fewer vibrations.

When to stop the brewing

Most kits just advise you to rack off the contents when the bubbles stop, or when the bubbling is running at a rate of one every 30 seconds or so. However, some are more exact in their instructions.

On rare occasions you might be asked to stop the brewing using a couple of crushed Campden tablets when the specific gravity has reached a particular level. Consequently you will need to use a hydrometer.

Using a hydrometer

Try to buy a hydrometer with a jar, not one on its own. The jar is used to hold the liquid. When you take some of your brew to test, make sure there are no bubbles in the beer before using the hydrometer itself. Then, make sure it is at room temperature too, because all the readings are standardised to what they call RT.

When you read the hydrometer, use the meniscus reading – the liquid will rise up the stem a little.

If the brew is at the correct reading, then stop the brewing using Campden tablets. A few hours later and all residual brewing will have stopped.

If your beer is intended for bottling, you do not need to kill the yeast with Campden tablets, but rather you will feed the yeast with a little sugar at the bottling stage.

How long does the brewing stage take?

It will take about 2 weeks for your brew to be 'ready' for the next stage. What that next stage is will depend on you, what you have used for your brewing vessel and the kind of brew you have made.

You might – as I often do – create a brew in a bucket, and then you simply scoop out the liquid with a large pail, but this is the desperate side of brewing. If you have a pressure vessel, the lees are usually left at the bottom of the barrel.

Bottling, which we looked at in Chapter 1, usually involves a secondary fermentation. You put a spoonful of sugar in your bottle before sealing it. This will produce a small secondary fermentation, creating a whole load of fizz.

MODIFYING A BEER KIT

Every year I make a special Christmas Beer, or punch, from a kit – but it's modified kit. This works best if you buy a brown ale or a stout, or if those two are not available, get yourself a mild beer kit.

When you have emptied the tin, save it if you can. I have a drainpipe made from such tins.

Before you start, remember that the alcohol produced in the brewing process becomes a preservative, but you can also grow bacteria and unwanted fungi in the brew. So make sure everything is sterile before use. The best way of doing this is with Milton or sterilising tablets, diluted appropriately.

Ingredients
To make 22.5 litres:

1 beer kit, as described
1 kg of glucose, from the chemist
Some nutmeg (yes, I do mean some – read on)
A handful of raisins
A handful of orange peel
250 g either of dark brown sugar, honey, treacle or golden syrup
1 cinnamon stick

Have ready a sterile fermentation bucket and lid

Method
- Use hot water to get the wort out of the can and into your brewing vessel, then add the kilo of glucose.
- Pour 2 litres of water into a large pan and add to it the extra sugar (whichever kind of sugar you decide on, as above), the raisins, the orange peel – I use about 3 oranges, and chop up the peel. Also a half teaspoon of nutmeg – which sounds a lot, but remember this is going to make 22.5 litres (although if you want less it's up to you) – and the cinnamon stick. Bring this to the boil and simmer for about 30 minutes.
- Pour this through a strainer into the wort, which is now cooling down in a large brewing bucket.
- Then top up to 25 litres with cold tap water. It is best if you use a proper brewing bucket with a lid, or a brewing cask. This way you just fill it to the 25 litre mark.
- Sprinkle the yeast on top of the liquid and pop the lid on. It's best to put this in a place where, should it spill, it won't create a complete mess. You can forget it for a week or two and within a few days it will have developed a scum on the top. This is because the protein in the liquid is forced to the surface by the gas bubbles. Remove the scum.

- After about three weeks the beer will have been brewed off completely, so if you are brewing this mid-November it will be ready about the end of the first week of December. You need to be sure your bottles are ready.
- Put a tablespoon of sugar into each bottle (or 2 tablespoons if you are using lemonade bottles) and carefully siphon off the beer. Seal and label the bottles.
- The bottles will become explosive when you open them, so do it over the sink and pour in a single steady operation so the sediment is not sprayed all over the place.
- Traditionally, this beer is served in a pewter pot into which a hot poker has been thrust to warm it up. There really is no better combination of sweetness, spice and booze. Alternatively you can heat it in a pan, and add another cinnamon stick for extra bite. The alcohol is quickly evaporated off, but the aroma of it gives you a warm feeling without intoxicating too much.

Variations to the standard kit

Instead of adding brewing sugar to the beer, why not try using malt instead? Use spray dried pale malt, or amber malt to add to your beer kit. This gives the beer a deeper, more developed and full-bodied flavour. Sugar itself adds no flavour, and since it is mostly brewed off, it is simply a source of alcohol. Spray malt is much to be preferred.

You can try combinations of malt: a three-way split of pale malt, amber malt and brewing sugar is one of my favourites. With this combination of malts, you get a darker brew (starting with a bitter kit) and the slightly increased protein in the spray malt gives the beer a longer lasting, more intense head.

MAKING YOUR OWN BEER KIT

There are lots of ways of making beer from very simple ingredients. You can buy from your brew shop ready-flavoured 'tea bags' filled with hops and other flavours which you just add to your wort. The secret is to be sure to use 500 g malt extract per 4.5 litres of water. This way you should have plenty of body in your beer without it being too strong. Here is a recipe for a simple home-made brew:

Ingredients
To make 22.5 litres:

> 2.5 kg pale malt extract
> 20 ordinary tea bags (with real tea in them – the kind you drink in a cup!)
> 500 g brewing sugar
> 1 brew bag
> Top fermenting beer yeast

Have ready a sterile fermentation vessel, muslin bag and airlock

Method
- Add all the ingredients to a large pan and boil for 30 minutes in about 2.5 litres of water.
- Sieve into a separate pan and sparge (wash the remaining solids with a kettle of hot water to get the last of the flavour out).
- Add to your brewing vessel, which already has some cold water in it, and top up to 22.5 litres with cold water. Check the temperature, and when it is between 18 and 21°C, add top fermenting beer yeast and fit your airlock.
- Allow to brew for two to three weeks then bottle in the usual way (see instructions on page 44).

Using liquid malt extract from the chemist

Yes, you can make good beer from the kind of malt extract you buy in the chemist's shop. Just make sure it doesn't have any cod liver oil in it. You need two and a half tins to make 22.5 litres of beer. Essentially, this malt extract needs sugar to get it brewing properly, and then some flavouring of some sort, otherwise the beer will taste weak and uninteresting. This is usually the starting point for some ancient reconstructions of ale from the Middle Ages, for example, the juice from half a bucket of dandelion leaves soaked in water makes a good brew.

Nettle beer

Nettles are an ancient way of flavouring beer. You should only take the tops of the nettle, to about 15 cm from the top of each stalk. This way you avoid the stronger flavours provided by the stringy stems beneath. This is a beer best brewed in springtime when the nettles are fresh.

Ingredients

To make 22.5 litres:

> 2.5 tins malt extract (the tins are usually 1 kg)
> 1 kg brewing sugar
> Enough nettles to fill a supermarket shopping bag (wear gloves to pick them!)
> Beer yeast

Have ready a sterile fermentation vessel and airlock

Method

- Boil your nettles in about 2 litres of water for about 20 minutes.
- Add the malt extract to your fermenting vessel, using hot water to dissolve it.

- Add the sugar and the nettle juice and top up to 22.5 litres.
- Check the temperature is 18–21°C
- Add the yeast and ferment with an airlock.
- Three weeks later, bottle in the usual way (see instructions on page 44).

CHAPTER 4

MAKING PALE ALE AND BITTER

Pale ale is our starting point for beer brewing as we venture forth in our journey from the lightest beers to the darkest. (I suppose Pilsner could have been first, but you can find out more about that beer in Chapter 7.)

It may come as a surprise to many people, but, pale ale is not really what we think it to be. When pale ale is mentioned, people often automatically think of India Pale Ale, now known as IPA, an export offshoot. Pale ale includes bitter beer, and was really an 18th century invention coming mostly from Burton on Trent. The story of what became the English pale ale style of beer really follows the Industrial Revolution quite closely – and marks the beginning of the change from people relying on home-brewed beers to mass-produced, though highly skilled, beer production.

Pale ale is also the first beer to be strongly commercialised. The red triangle of Bass beers was the first ever registered trademark, and this went around the world as a marketed product. With pale ale, beer became a mass-marketed product – beer was now big business.

As with other industries at the very start of the Industrial Revolution, wood was used as a fuel for roasting barley. Being rich in resins, wood always produced a dark roasted malt – and consequently a dark beer. This was the ale and beer of the working man, brewed in the beer shed, in a copper.

Bass Brewery was founded by William Bass in 1777 in Burton on Trent. Situated as they were at the very epicentre of the Industrial Revolution, the brewers soon discovered that roasting with coke rather than wood produced a very light malt and the appropriate amber beer.

The main difference was that the wood-roasted barley had a smoky flavour which was transferred to the brew, though in a much diluted form. By comparison, most bitters and pale ales were produced to be quite hoppy in flavour, reasonably low in alcohol and not too highly carbonated. (Although using the phrase 'not too highly carbonated' implies that carbon dioxide was added later, this, obviously, was not the case.)

There was something about the water of the Trent that gave the beers of Burton a special flavour. The water is particularly hard, and contains a lot of dissolved salts. In particular the brew made with this water is able to withstand a higher hop content, and in turn this preserves the beer better.

When the railway appeared at Burton on Trent, Bass's pale ale was exported around the world, following the expansion of the Empire – which, after all, had at its heart an awful lot of thirsty soldiers!

INDIA PALE ALE

There are a number of myths about India Pale Ale, but it actually came about as the result of a number of commercial difficulties. Many countries put taxes on imported beer, and so the Burton group of brewers lost their markets, especially in Russia. At the same time, the East India Company found that it did not have the ability to brew beer in India, and so was on the lookout for a strongly hopped, slightly more alcoholic beer, which would last the long and vigorous voyage to India from the UK.

India Pale Ale was slightly altered October beer, a drink high in alcohol, brewed in country houses and set in the cellar for a long time. It was thought the high alcohol content would keep the beer on its long journey to the subcontinent, and consequently the ale was bought in great quantity. The label India Pale Ale evolved over a number of years.

MAKING PALE ALE

You can recreate the authentic flavour of Burton water by adding Burton salts. This is a mixture of gypsum, potassium chloride and Epsom salts. A standard 800 g container will last a year or more of brewing – depending on how thirsty you are! You only need about a teaspoon per five gallons, and it should be added right at the start of the brewing process. However, if you prefer, you can brew pale ale very successfully without adding the salts.

The difference between extracted and grain brewing is immense in one way, but completely the same in another. The difference being that the extracted mash from the wort is poured off and sparged, that is, to rinse off the remaining wort 'clinging' to the grain.

What's the difference in practice? Almost none, you can get excellent beers from both methods, and at the end of the day, it is what goes into the glass that counts. However, pale ale is often brewed from grains because the extract is darkened in production.

Making sure your pint has a good head

Bitter beers often have a good head on them, whereas pale ale doesn't necessarily have a head at all. If you're looking for a good head on your pale ale, the way to be sure of one is to throw a handful of torrified wheat into the wort at boiling. This increases the protein enough to catch the bubbles.

MAKING EASY BITTER BEER FROM EXTRACT

Actually, I call this gardener's bitter – it's just the stuff to wash away the dust and toil of a day's gardening! Here is an extract recipe that produces a beer that is about 3.6% alcohol, and quite tasty to boot.

Ingredients
To make 22.5 litres:

2.3 kg pale malt extract
350 g crystal malt
75 g Goldings hops
Top fermenting beer yeast

Have ready a sterile fermentation vessel and airlock

Method
- Bring 4 litres of water to the boil, then add the malts and 50 g of the hops. Boil for 55 mins, then add the rest of the Goldings

hops and boil for another 5 minutes to complete one hour's boiling time altogether.

- Pour 18.5 litres of cold water into a fermenting vessel, then strain the wort and add that in.
- Check the temperature is in the range of 18–21°C and then pitch the yeast.
- Allow the yeast to grow for four days, removing any foam that appears, and then fit an airlock.
- Ferment the sugar out until it stops bubbling. The final gravity should be 1.010 or thereabouts, so pretty much all the sugar is used up!

This is a great one to brew in a tapped vessel, as there isn't a great deal of sediment and what there is simply remains below the tap. Of course, the vessel needs to be undisturbed! If you're not using a tapped vessel, you can simply siphon your beer off into another vessel or keg, and then bottle in the normal way (see instructions on page 44).

MAKING BITTER BEER

We have already said the difference between ale and beer is hops, but by the time pale ale was introduced, the terms had become very much intertwined. Ale became the name for rich dark brews and beer was the name given to lighter brews, especially this version using pale malt.

Ingredients
To make 22.5 litres:

2.5 kg crushed pale malt
150 g crushed crystal malt
75 g Fuggles hops

25 g Goldings hops
500 g brewing sugar
Top fermenting beer yeast

Have ready a sterile fermentation vessel, muslin bag and airlock

Method

- Place 3 litres of water in a large pan with both the malts and bring to the boil. This is to be simmered for an hour.
- Strain the brew into a fermenting bin, through a muslin which will catch the debris.
- Sparge the remaining hops to remove the rest of the sugar and flavour. (Sparging means to wash it through with hot water. The sparging water goes into your brew.)
- Add the spent hops to the pan and add the sugar and a couple of litres of water. Boil for 15 minutes and then pour through the muslin back into the fermenting bin.
- Make up to 22.5 litres with cold water and check the temperature. You are looking for the beer to be in the range of 18–21°C.
- Sprinkle the yeast on the surface.
- Over the course of about a week a foam will keep appearing on the surface of the beer, which should be skimmed off. After about a week the beer can be racked, that is, siphoned off the lees (dead yeast) into another fermenting vessel or keg.
- You can then bottle after another week (see instructions on page 44), or leave it in the keg. The beer will be ready to drink in about another fortnight.

MAKING A SIMPLE PALE ALE USING EXTRACT

This has to be one of the easiest recipes you can find for beer, and it really does work well – giving you a vigorous fermentation and a strong, flavoursome brew. The Goldings hops provide a smooth sweet aroma.

Ingredients
To make 22.5 litres:

2 kg dried pale malt extract
1 kg brewing sugar
60 g crystal malt
100 g Goldings hops
Beer yeast

Have ready a sterile fermentation vessel, muslin bag and airlock

Method
- This beer is easily made, just boil everything except the yeast and sugar in 5 litres of water for an hour.
- Pour the wort through a muslin into a fermentation vessel and stir in the sugar. Sparge the remaining hops with a kettle of water and then fill the vessel to 22.5 litres.
- Check the temperature, and when it is between 18–21°C you can then sprinkle the beer yeast on the surface.
- Over the course of about five days, remove any foam that arises, and then transfer to either another keg or to a vessel which can have an airlock fitted. I tend to divide my brew equally into five demijohns for ease of use later.
- About two weeks later the brew will be ready for bottling (see instructions on page 44), and in another month you will have great pale ale.

MAKING PALE ALE

Ingredients
To make 22.5 litres:

  2.5 kg crushed pale malt
  1 kg brewing sugar
  125 g crystal malt
  100 g Goldings hops
  Top fermenting beer yeast

Have ready a sterile fermentation vessel, muslin bag and airlock

Method
- Soak the grains in 5 litres of water and the crystal malt for an hour at 60°C and then add the hops to make your mash.
- Bring to the boil and then allow to cool before straining through a muslin into another vessel. Add your sugar and make up to 22.5 litres with cold water.
- Add the yeast and over the course of about a week remove any foam that appears. Then fit an airlock, or transfer the brew to another vessel with an airlock fitted.
- Ten days later you can clear with finings and then rack off into another vessel.
- Before bottling, prime the beer. That is, add sugar for a secondary fermentation in the bottle. Use 125 g brewing sugar dissolved in a cup of warm water.
- Bottle your brew (see instructions on page 44) and then store it for at least a month.

MAKING INDIA PALE ALE

This is a strong ale which is easy to make, but might be a little too hoppy in flavour for some. It takes a while to mature in the bottle, but is very much worth the wait.

Originally, of course, crystal malt would not have been in IPA because it would not have been invented at the time. The crystal malt does add a richness of colour – but try it without if you like, just add some brewing sugar instead.

Ingredients
To make 22.5 litres:

> 3 kg pale malt extract
> 1 kg amber malt extract
> 0.5 kg crystal malt
> 125 g Goldings hops
> Top fermenting beer yeast

Have ready a sterile fermentation vessel, muslin bag and airlock

Method
- Steep the crystal malt in 5 litres of water at 60°C for 30 minutes, then pour off the liquid into a fermenting bin.
- Boil the malt extract for 60 minutes in 5 litres of water, adding the hops for the last 30 minutes.
- Allow the liquid to cool and then strain through a muslin into the fermenting vessel.
- Make up to 22.5 litres with cold water and then add top fermenting beer yeast.
- Over the course of about a week, remove any foam that appears, then fit an airlock or transfer the brew to an air-locked container.

- Clear, rack and bottle (see instructions on page 44) after a further two weeks.

MAKING LIGHT PALE ALE

Don't be fooled by this beer, it is not light in the alcohol department, but it does show the technique of varying the use of hops to get a number of flavours and a bright sharp hop to the beer.

If you boil hops for a long time you lose some of the bright tones you would have if you only boiled them for a minute or two, and so varying the hop in the brew gives a very different balance.

The recipe also calls for wheat malt, giving this beer a grassy flavour.

Ingredients
To make 22.5 litres:

  2 kg pale malt
  1 kg wheat malt
  125 g crystal malt
  100 g Goldings hops (divide into 3 equal parts)
  Top fermenting beer yeast

Have ready a sterile fermentation vessel, muslin bag and airlock

Method
- Soak the grains and the crystal malt in 8 litres of water for an hour at 60°C to make your mash. (You need a big pan for this.)
- Bring to the boil and add the first amount of hops. Boil for 45 minutes, then the next amount of hops, continuing the boil for 15 minutes. Finally add the last of the hops and boil for 5 minutes.

- Allow to cool before filtering into another vessel. Then make up to 22.5 litres with cold water.
- Check the temperature. If it is between 18 and 21°C, add the yeast.
- Over the course of about a week, remove any foam that appears, then fit an airlock, or transfer the brew to another vessel with an airlock fitted.
- Ten days later you can clear with finings and then rack off into another vessel.
- Before bottling, prime the beer. That is, add sugar for a secondary fermentation in the bottle. Use 125 g brewing sugar in a cup of warm water.
- Bottle your beer (see instructions on page 44) and then store for at least a month.

MAKING WHEAT BEER

These are not actually pale ales at all. It has been suggested that wheat has been used for beer making for a long time; much longer than malted barley. Wheat beers are mainly from northern Europe, and most famously from Germany, where they are called Weizen (wheat) Bier.

Wheat is not so rich in the enzymes that cause the transformation of starch into sugar, and so the malted wheat is nearly always mixed with barley in the mash. The mix is nearly always 40% barley and 60% wheat.

Malted wheat is made pretty much in the same way as malted barley, and you can buy it more readily these days. More importantly, you can buy wheat extract in liquid and dry form, so the making of a wheat beer is not out of the question.

Ingredients

To make 22.5 litres:

2.5 kg wheat extract

1 kg pale malt extract

500 g brewing sugar

75 g Saaz hops (divided into two equal halves)

1 packet Hefeweizen yeast

Have ready a sterile fermentation vessel, muslin bag and airlock

Method

- Bring the wheat, malt and sugar to the boil in about 2–3 litres of water. After 20 minutes add half the hops. After another 15 minutes add the other half and boil for a further 15 minutes.
- Strain through a muslin into a fermentation vessel and then add cold water to make it up to 22.5 litres.
- Check the temperature – this beer works best at lower temperatures, about 18°C is best. Then add your yeast.
- After about three days fit an airlock and ferment until the bubbles stop.
- Rack off and then bottle (see instructions on page 44). This beer is best after it has been kept for about a month.

MAKING ALL GRAIN WHEAT BEER

Ingredients

To make 22.5 litres:

2 kg wheat malt

1 kg pale malt

50 g Saaz hops (divided into 2 equal parts)

1 packet Hefeweizen yeast

Have ready a sterile fermentation vessel and airlock

Method
- Steep all the grains for 60 minutes at 66°C.
- Drain the liquid into a large pan and sparge the remaining grains 4 or 5 times with hot water into the pan.
- Bring to the boil. After 15 minutes add half the hops. After another 10 minutes add the rest of the hops, then boil for a further 10 minutes.
- Bring up to 22.5 litres with cold water and then check the temperature. This likes to be at around 18°C, so once the brew reaches that temperature you can pitch the yeast.
- After about three days fit an airlock and ferment until the bubbles stop.
- Rack off and then bottle (see instructions on page 44). This beer is best after it has been kept for about a month.

CHAPTER 5

MAKING MILD BEER

When I was a young beer drinker, complete with rustic tweed jacket, leather elbow patches and the occasional cigar, my drink of choice was a brown split. A brown split is a half pint of mild and a brown ale. Thinking myself somehow sophisticated, in a 1950s sort of way, I imagined the rich dark liquid in my pot to be somehow contemplative and solid.

Actually, nothing could be further from the truth!

First of all, mild beer was never a really strong drink (unless you count those produced in the early 19th century) but was supposed to be an easy beer to drink to slake your thirst.

Secondly, in brewing terms, the bottle of brown ale with which I enhanced my half pint of mild, was actually, in brewing terms, pretty much the same thing.

Rather than being sophisticated, mild beer was a drinker's drink. It was very much a miner's or mill worker's drink and indeed, there are old photographs of beer sellers waiting outside Lancashire mills, selling mild beer to the workers coming out of the factory at the end of a hard day's work.

In the north of England mild beer is sometimes less dark than in the south, and there used to be a progression of beer colour, getting darker as you continued south.

Mild beer is made from pale malt mixed with darker malt or roasted grains to provide the darker colour. Before the First World War, this brew was stronger than it is today, but the government brought out a number of arrangements to reduce the alcohol content, and restrict the price.

The changes made mild beer less popular, and in recent years it has been almost completely replaced by lager and bitter. Recent sales figures from pubs show that mild represents around 1% of all beer sold, and there are many pubs that simply do not sell mild at all.

Traditionally, there wasn't much in the way of hops in mild beer, and the overriding flavour was malt. In recent years mild has had something of a resurgence in microbreweries. Particularly strong dark beers are being produced under the name mild, but in fact these are not 'mild' at all!

What difference do the hops make? Well, many of the recipes call for Goldings hops, but Fuggles hops give a grassier flavour. There are a number of milds that are brewed with a 50:50 mix of Goldings and Fuggles.

It is about time that mild beer should come back to popularity, particularly as it is an easy beer to drink. Quite why it has been largely replaced by lager as a young person's drink I cannot fathom, because it is a much safer brew. Perhaps that is the knuckle of the matter?

NUT BROWN ALE

This is more of a description than a kind of brown ale. The name comes from the use of heavily roasted barley and crystal malt, with a low hop content. The result is a subtle pint in which the flavours of the barley, and their caramelised roasting, come to the fore rather than the overpowering flavour of hops.

MAKING A REALLY SIMPLE MILD

Ingredients
To make 5 litres:

500 g dark malt extract
100 g cracked crystal malt
25 g Fuggles hops
Top fermenting beer yeast

Have ready a sterile bucket, demijohn, bung and airlock

Method
- Place all the ingredients, except of course the yeast, in a pan with 2.5 litres of water and bring to the boil. Simmer for 30 minutes and then strain the liquid into a bucket to cool.
- Sparge the remaining hops with 500 ml warm water into the bucket.
- When quite cool, transfer the liquid to a demijohn, top up to the neck with cold water and add a teaspoon of yeast.

- Leave for five days without an airlock, then fit an airlock and leave to ferment for a couple of weeks, by which time the bubbles should have stopped. Place the demijohn in a bowl to catch any spillage that comes out of the top.
- Rack off into a second demijohn, add 2 tablespoons of sugar dissolved in warm water to sparkle the beer, and then bottle (see instructions on page 44). Wait for two weeks or so before drinking, but as with most mild beer, nothing is gained by leaving it longer.
- Try modifying this by adding 450 g honey to the wort – this makes a really special set of interesting flavours.

Making a larger quantity of mild

Clearly, you need a larger brewing vessel to achieve this, but the principles are the same.

Ingredients

To make 22.5 litres:

> 1.5 kg dark malt extract
> 300 g cracked crystal malt
> 100 g Fuggles hops
> 1 tablespoon molasses
> Top fermenting beer yeast

Have ready a sterile fermentation vessel, muslin bag and airlock

Method

- The brewing process is exactly the same as for the smaller quantity.
- Bring the ingredients, except of course the yeast, to the boil in 4.5 litres of water. Sparge in the normal way and then make up to 22.5 litres with cold water. Note the temperature – keep in a warm place if necessary until it attains 18–21°C.

- Leave for a week and then transfer to a vessel that has an airlock – or fit one to the vessel you are using. During the first week, remove any foam that is produced.
- Bottle in the normal way (see instructions on page 44).

MAKING BROWN ALE

It has been the method of many brewers to add all kinds of malt to brown ale to get a kind of colour/flavour balance that was 'just right'. I started by using molasses, having completely the wrong idea, but the brewing process is so forgiving anyway that I enjoyed the brew – even if no one else did.

I ended up, after some experimentation, with a brew that was about 1/5 crystal malt and 4/5 pale malt. I use ordinary brewing sugar too, and you get a full-bodied brown ale, even if it is still mostly pale malt.

Ingredients
To make 22.5 litres:

   3 kg crushed pale malt grain
   600 g crystal malt
   450 g brewing sugar
   100 g Goldings hops
   Top fermenting beer yeast

Have ready a sterile fermentation vessel, muslin bag and airlock

Method
- Steep the pale malt and the crystal malt at 65°C for 90 minutes and stir often. Try to keep the temperature constant – I use hot towels as a heat source.

- Pour off the wort and sparge the remaining grains with a kettle of hot water.
- Add the sugar and hops and then bring to the boil.
- Bring up to 22.5 litres with cold water and check the temperature. When it is between 18–21°C add the yeast and cover.
- Over the course of five days, remove any foam that appears, then fit an airlock.
- Ferment for three weeks and rack off. This needs to be bottled almost straight away (see instructions on page 44), and consumed fairly quickly too.

Making an even darker brown ale

If you substitute the malts in the previous recipe with the same amount of dark malt, use 1 kg of brewing sugar, and replace the Goldings hops with Fuggles, you will have a wonderfully dark brown brew which is guaranteed to turn you into a folk singer.

Darkening other recipes

If you really want a dark drink but cannot get dark malt, then use a tablespoon of gravy browning, or caramel if you can't get it. This will make your brew quite brown. I like also to add some dark sugar too. In fact, the darker the sugars the better the flavours.

Be careful, though, as you are in danger of growing a beard when drinking too much brown ale, and your jackets will mysteriously sprout leather patches on the elbows.

MAKING MILD BEER WITH CHOCOLATE MALT

You can make a dark brew using pale malt with a little chocolate malt. This is a really easy brew that gives a great result. You will find the dark brown sugar adds a real richness – you can also try a little molasses instead!

The point is that you are creating richness – think liver and bacon, or black pudding. It's quite rewarding to experiment with this beer.

Ingredients
To make 22.5 litres:

2.25 kg pale malt extract
300 g chocolate malt extract
300 g dark brown sugar
300 g crystal malt
100 g Goldings hops
Top fermenting beer yeast

Have ready a sterile fermentation vessel and airlock

Method
- Boil the sugar and the malts in about 4 litres of water for 45 minutes. During the last 15 minutes add the hops and then transfer the liquid to a fermenting vessel and bring up to 22.5 litres with cold water.
- Check the temperature and if it is in the range of 18–21°C you can pitch the yeast.
- Leave for four days before adding the airlock. It should be brewed out within a fortnight.
- Bottle in the normal way (see instructions on page 44).

MAKING EASY GUINNESS

This wondrous brew is included here because although it is a dark ale, it is not all that strong. You can drink gallons of the stuff and maintain the vertical attitude – only an increased number of visits to the toilet and a wonderfully nourished, happy feeling will show that you have been drinking the stuff.

Of course, the majority of the flavour comes from the yeast, so you have to use Irish ale yeast, which is readily available. When you brew in a fermenting vessel, the dead yeast falls as the lees. It is a light brown colour and in the brewing industry it is boiled with salt to make Marmite. (I made some Marmite once – but don't bother trying to do it yourself as it's not that brilliant.) Not all of this yeast is dead, and if you refrigerate it, a couple of tablespoons can be used to set your next batch going.

However, do not continue this process time and again because the yeast has a higher chance of becoming contaminated with other microbes that you wouldn't want in your beer.

Ingredients
To make 22.5 litres:

    3 kg pale malt
    1 kg dark malt extract
    1 kg flaked barley
    75 g Northern Brewers hops
    1 packet Irish ale yeast

Have ready a sterile fermentation vessel, muslin bag and airlock

Method

- Soak the pale malt and the flaked barley at 66°C for 60 minutes in 3 litres of water.
- Drain into a pan and sparge the remaining solids 4 times into the pan. Bring to the boil and add the dark malt extract.
- Boil for 15 minutes then add 25 g hops. Boil for another 15 minutes then add another 25 g of the hops. Boil for another 15 minutes then add the final 25 g of hops. Then boil for a final 15 minutes.
- Strain the liquid into a fermenting vessel and make up to 22.5 litres.
- Check the temperature and if it is between 18–21°C pitch your yeast.
- Leave uncovered for four days, removing any foam that appears, then fit an airlock for the remaining couple of weeks of fermenting time.
- Rack off when the bubbles stop. Then add 125 g of sugar dissolved in a cup of boiling water before bottling on the following day (see instructions on page 44).

CHAPTER 6

MAKING STOUT AND STRONG ALES

When young master Ben was born, his father put down some ale, to be opened when Ben came of age – this is the tradition of strong ale. It wasn't until the late 18th century that these ales were seriously brewed commercially, partly because they were expensive, partly because they were an acquired taste and partly because they were so strong. Some of them were over 10% proof.

This group of beers includes porter, stout and barley wine, but not Guinness – which is not a strong ale, but rather a food rich session beer of average to low strength. Many strong ales are dark in colour.

In commercial terms the word stout means strong, and it was produced from the mid-17th century. For some reason known only to history, stout was enjoyed by the porters working on the Thames in London. In one of the ale houses on the river, the nickname 'porter' was given to the favourite beer of the porters for the ferry, and the name stuck. In the early 1720s, the name porter was used for the strongest of stouts.

Made from roasted malt, the early porters were an acquired taste because the malt roasting process often produced burned and awkward flavours. These flavours were replaced in the nineteenth century by using a combination of malt and roasted grains. Also, as we have already seen, the roasting processes improved when brewers began using coke as a fuel. This was much less smoky than the wood fuel that was previously used, and produced a really clean malt.

ORIGINAL GRAVITY

The magic figure of 1090 produces a drink that is over 10% alcohol when all is fermented out. This is the figure needed to ensure the beer will stay preserved in the bottle, needing no other preservatives. Consequently, strong ales are not all that hoppy in character but thick and rich.

MAKING PORTER USING MALT EXTRACT

This is great left in the barrel. You do need to rack it once, and you can also clear it with finings if you want to – though I never bother.

Ingredients
To make 22.5 litres:

2 kg dark malt extract
300 g cracked crystal malt
300 g crushed black malt
125 g Fuggles hops
1 kg brewing sugar
Top fermenting beer yeast

Have ready a sterile fermentation vessel, muslin bag and airlock

Method
- Simply bring the ingredients, except of course the yeast, to the boil in about 4 litres of water, and boil for 30 minutes.
- Strain the liquid into a fermenting vessel and sparge the remaining solids.
- Top up to 22.5 litres with cold water and check the temperature is between 18 and 21°C before pitching the yeast.
- Leave for four days, removing any foam that appears, before adding an airlock.
- After another couple of weeks of fermentation you are ready to rack and clear. If you are going to bottle then add a teaspoon of sugar to each, to sparkle the beer (see instructions on page 44). Drink as soon as possible.

MAKING STOUT

This one calls for pale malt, but you are going to considerably darken it, using additional black malt and dark brown sugar.

Ingredients
To make 22.5 litres:

2.2 kg pale malt (dried extract)
300 g ground black malt

500 g dark brown sugar
125 g Fuggles hops
Top fermenting beer yeast

Have ready a sterile fermentation vessel, muslin bag and airlock

Method
- Boil all the ingredients, except of course the yeast, for 45 minutes, in 4.4 litres of water. Also keep back 25 g of the hops until the last 5 minutes of the boiling.
- Strain into a fermenting vessel that already has 17 litres of cold water in it.
- Sparge the remaining solids with boiling water and add to the liquid.
- Check the temperature is in the range 18–21°C. Then pitch your yeast and leave it to ferment for about a week. Remove any foam that accumulates and then add your airlock.
- The stout will be fermented out in another 7–10 days.
- Bottle in the usual way (see instructions on page 44).

You can thicken the head characteristics by adding a handful of torrified wheat, or some roasted barley, to the initial boil.

MAKING MILK STOUT

When I was a boy I used to visit my grandmother for the weekend, and my uncle would always return from an evening out smelling of beer. We had a ritual: I asked him what he had been drinking and he replied, 'milk'. It was many years before I realised he meant milk stout.

This drink puzzled me for a long time – how could they make beer from milk? The truth is the stout is fortified with milk sugar, lactose. Yeast cannot ferment lactose, and so the beer is mildly sweetened.

Milk stout was said to be nutritious, and used to be given to nursing mothers. Mackeson is an example of milk stout.

MAKING A MACKESON CLONE

Well, this might not be exactly how they brew it, but it is close. You'll be saying, 'It looks good . . . it tastes good . . .' – just like the old chap on the old advert!

Ingredients
To make 22.5 litres:

   3 kg pale malt extract
   500 g chocolate malt
   250 g black patent malt
   500 g lactose
   50 g Northern Brewer hops
   Good quality beer yeast – ask in your brew shop for ale yeast

Have ready a sterile fermentation vessel and airlock

Method
- Steep the grains at 64°C in 5 litres of water.
- Strain into a second pan and sparge the remaining solids.
- Bring to the boil, add the malt extract and the lactose and boil for 45 minutes, adding the hops after 15 minutes.
- Add water to make up to 22.5 litres in a fermenting bin.
- Check the temperature is between 18 and 21°C and then pitch the yeast.
- Allow to grow for five days, removing any foam and then add your airlock. Ferment out for a week to ten days.
- Bottle in the usual way, with a teaspoon of sugar per bottle (see instructions on page 44). This will keep for ages, and you will

get a deposit in the beer too, so you have to pour like an Englishman!

How to pour like an Englishman

Actually, it's not just the English. . . but pouring beer used to involve a technique that would today be frowned upon. Certainly, the current habit of drinking beer from the bottle would never, ever have been allowed some 30 years ago. Bottles were often stored in the pub yard, and any cat might pee on them – that's what an old chap said to me in my student days when he saw me drinking from a bottle, though he didn't say pee.

Then, of course, when you tip a bottle of stout, the sediment is disturbed. So, to pour this type of beer, you have to do it in one movement, and do not right the bottle at all during the process. You also leave a little liquid in the bottle with the remaining sediment.

MAKING BARLEY WINE

This brew is about the simplest you can get and it is a really light one, though quite alcoholic – easy and simple really!

Ingredients

To make 4.5 litres:

500 g barley grains
500 g raisins
Juice of 2 lemons
1.5 kg brewing sugar
Teaspoon of turbo yeast (high alcohol)
Half a teaspoon of pectolase (to help get more juice and sugars from the raisins)

Have ready a sterile fermenting vessel, demijohn, bung and airlock

Method

- Chop the raisins and mix with the barley grains. Place them in a pan and pour 3 litres of boiling water over them, and leave to stand for 24 hours.
- Add the liquid to a clean fermenting vessel and make up to 5 litres with boiling water.
- Add the rest of the ingredients except the yeast and stir well.
- After three days of regular stirring, strain into a demijohn and pitch the yeast, fit an airlock and allow to ferment to completion.
- Add a Campden tablet when the bubbles stop and then rack into a clean demijohn. I keep this for a couple of months and pour from the demijohn rather than bottling it.

MAKING BARLEY WINE FROM EXTRACT

Ingredients
To make 10 litres:

2.25 kg pale malt extract
500 g crystal malt
25 g Fuggles hops
Juice of 2 lemons
Top fermenting beer yeast

Have ready two sterile demijohns, bungs and airlocks

Method

- Steep the crystal malt in 2 litres of water at 65°C for an hour. Pour off the liquid into a pan and then sparge the remaining solids too.

- Add the rest of the ingredients and 4 litres of water and boil for 45 minutes.
- Cool the wort and share equally between two demijohns. Top up with cooled boiled water.
- Pitch your yeast and allow the brew to complete – fitting an airlock to each of your demijohns.
- When the bubbles stop, add a Campden tablet to each demijohn and rack off.
- You can bottle this powerful brew in small bottles –there is no need to add sugar. It tastes wonderful! (See instructions for bottling on page 44.)

MAKING HONEYED BEER

The thing about honey is that it is only 80% sugar, and consequently, you have to take this into account. But it is not just sugar you are adding; honey has its own pleasant flavour. I am always surprised at the refreshing nature of this brew. It is golden and strong – just the stuff to invoke an afternoon's sleep in the garden. Mead producers simply use the hydrometer to get the right amount of sugar in the brew. The torrified wheat is there to make sure there is a good head on the beer.

Ingredients
To make 22.5 litres:

> 3 kg pale malt extract
> 750 g honey
> 75 g Northern Brewer hops
> 25 g Goldings hops
> A handful of torrified wheat
> Good quality beer yeast

Have ready a sterile fermentation vessel and airlock

Method

- Add the malt to about 4 litres of water and bring to the boil. Simmer for 30 minutes and then add the honey, torrified wheat and hops, and simmer for another 15 minutes, stirring all the time to make sure the honey is completely dissolved.
- Add water to make up to 22.5 litres in a fermenting bin.
- Check the temperature is between 18 and 21°C and then pitch your yeast.
- Allow to grow for five days, removing any foam that appears, and then add your airlock.
- Ferment out for a week to ten days.
- When the bubbles have stopped, rack off and bottle (see instructions on page 44).

CHAPTER 7

MAKING LAGER

If ever a drink came from nobility, it was lager. All over Europe, the UK included, people brewed their own beer. Great houses in the UK brewed in the summer time and stored the beer the rest of the year. In the high Bavarian Alps people had difficulty in finding good storage conditions for their beer, partly because it was cold.

Consequently, experimentation with cooler acting yeast produced a beer that matured at lower temperatures. Continued experimentation included removing much of the colour out of the beer, and lager beer was born.

The term Lager is German for storage (I suppose we should call it larder beer, which would be a more accurate description).

Pale beer became very popular across Europe in the nineteenth century, and lager was brewed in countries including Germany,

Belgium, Austria and Bohemia – where the name Pilsner first came about.

THE CHARACTERISTICS OF LAGER

High carbonation

When you dissolve a gas in a liquid, the process is more effective if the liquid is cold. You can dissolve a lot more carbon dioxide in cool water (beer) than if it is warm. Consequently, lager beer is high in gas, and modern factory brewers actually use liquid carbon dioxide to gas the beer.

Lack of colour or sediment

Lager has become paler, as this was a measure of how good the brewer was, and consequently how much he could charge. The process involves two fermentations: a general ferment, much the same as today's home brew; and then a lengthy secondary, or lagering fermentation.

During the months in cold caves the lager would settle and clear, creating a light colour. Of course, the malt also had a role to play in this process. Pilsner malt was roasted at such low temperatures, it hardly changed colour.

Over the years, lager has become ubiquitous – everyone seems to drink the chemicalised, under-stored, gassed up, filtered, tasteless, weak beer that passes for lager. Rest assured, your brew at home will be much better!

Lager from around the world

In just the same way as pale ales and bitter dislodged mild beer from its position of popularity, lager has done much the same. The beer was spread around Europe partially on the back of travelling armies. Lager quickly became the popular beer in Europe and then spread to America, where a series of quite individual beers developed.

The spread of American culture has meant that lager is now consumed and made on every continent, and even countries that have a no-alcohol policy brew it for visitors, to be drunk in specially controlled situations.

MAKING A REALLY EASY LAGER

This recipe uses a can of lager malt that has already been hopped. In short, it uses a lager kit, though we are going to modify it!

Ingredients
To make 22.5 litres:

> 1 lager kit
> 750 g pale malt extract
> 4 tea bags (I prefer Yorkshire tea – but anything other than Earl Grey will do)
> 25 g Goldings hops
> Bottom fermenting yeast (often the kit will have the appropriate yeast)

Have ready a sterile fermentation vessel, muslin bag and airlock

Method
- Dissolve the wort from the kit in 4.5 litres of boiling water. Boil for 20 minutes and add the pale malt.

- Boil for a further 20 minutes and strain into a fermenting vessel with 18 litres of cold water in it.
- Tie the tea bags and the hops into a piece of muslin and add to the wort. Stir well.
- Leave for 24 hours, stirring occasionally. Remove the bag.
- Check the temperature and if it is in the range of 18–21°C pitch your yeast.
- Allow to ferment until the bubbles stop. You might want to use finings to help clear it at this point, but you then rack off into another vessel and add 125 g sugar in a cup of boiling water.
- Leave in the garage, shed or other cool place for a month before bottling (see instructions on page 44).

MAKING LAGER USING SAAZ HOPS

Ingredients
To make 22.5 litres:

> 2 kg pale malt extract
> 500 g brewing sugar
> 75 g Saaz hops
> Lager yeast

Have ready a sterile fermentation vessel, muslin bag and airlock

Method
- Dissolve the hops and the malt in 4.5 litres of water and add the sugar when you bring the lot to the boil. Boil for 30 minutes.
- Strain off the liquid into a fermenting vessel and sparge the remaining solids with a kettle of hot water.
- Make up to 22.5 litres with cold water. Check the temperature and, if it is between 18 and 21°C, pitch the yeast.

- Leave to grow in aerated water for three days, then fit the airlock.
- Leave to brew out and then rack off into a second vessel, charge with half a cup of corn sugar in a cup of hot water, and then keep it in the garage, shed or other cool place for a month.
- Bottle in the normal way (see instructions on page 44).

MAKING LAGER USING FLAKED MAIZE

This is a great lager to make, using flaked corn. In truth you can substitute cornflakes, but the difference is that cornflakes are a bit more roasted than brewing quality corn.

There are lots of recipes, including using rice and wheat, but the recipe below is the easiest in that it gives consistent results.

The other hops commonly used in lager are Hallertauer, which is listed in this recipe. If you cannot get it, try Saaz, or if you are having really bad shopping luck, try the best Goldings hops you can get your hands on.

Ingredients
To make 22.5 litres:

2.25 kg crushed Pilsner malt
200 g flaked maize
50 g Hallertauer hops
25 g Goldings hops
Lager yeast

Have ready a sterile fermentation vessel, muslin bag and airlock

Method

- This is a proper mash method. Add the Pilsner malt and the corn to a pan and pour lukewarm water over it until you have a porridge consistency.
- Heat to 66°C and leave for an hour – cover with a hot towel to keep the temperature even. Then raise the temperature back to 66°C and allow to cool.
- Strain off the liquid through a muslin cloth into a pan and sparge the remaining solids with lukewarm water until you have a good 10 litres of wort.
- Probably you will need two batches for this next stage. Bring the wort to the boil and add the Hallertauer hops, boil for 30 minutes, then add the Goldings hops and boil for another 15 minutes or so.
- Strain the liquid into a fermenting vessel and make up to 22.5 litres with cold water.
- Check the temperature is between 18 and 21°C and then pitch the yeast. Leave open (covered with a towel) for four days, and then fit an airlock.
- When the fermentation has stopped, rack off and store in a barrel for a month in a cold garage or shed. Bottle in the usual way (see instructions on page 44).

MAKING DARK LAGER

Everything I have said about lager being a pale drink is actually a lie. The problem is that lager is universally known as a pale drink, so once we have that idea out of our heads, we can go back to the beginnings of lager as it was brewed in Munich.

This recipe is a bit like a brown ale, but has Hallertauer hops and lager yeast. Remember that it is the yeast that adds a lot of the flavour.

Ingredients

To make 22.5 litres:

2.5 kg dark malt extract
200 g crushed crystal malt
100 g Hallertauer hops
Lager yeast

Have ready a sterile fermentation vessel, muslin bag and airlock

Method

- Bring the malts to the boil in 2 litres of water, and then boil for 30 minutes. Add the hops and then boil for another 15 minutes.
- Strain into a fermentation vessel, and top up with water to make 22.5 litres.
- Check the temperature and if it is between 18 and 21°C, add the lager yeast.
- Add the airlock straight away and ferment until the bubbles stop.
- Rack off into another vessel and then add 125 g brewing sugar in a cup of boiling water.
- Leave in a cold garage or shed for a month. You can then bottle or cask your lager (see instructions on page 44).

CHAPTER 8

MAKING CIDER AND PERRY

Cider making is so much easier than beer making. It is really a kind of wine making, and is particularly Celtic in origin. The variations in cider – dry, sweet, sparkling and so on – are more or less a function of the mixes of fruit that you use.

There is no malt in cider, and consequently no variation depending on how the malt is roasted. But perhaps more importantly, there is no sugar. Well, technically there is, as the sugar comes from the apples. There is a huge debate about the adding of sugar to cider, with the general consensus being that it shouldn't be done.

There is an enormous history of cider making in this country that goes back hundreds, if not thousands of years. It is one of the wonders of nature that cider is simple to make and very good for you to boot. The old adage, an apple a day keeps the doctor away, certainly applies to cider.

The main health benefits of cider have long been associated with antioxidants. These compounds mop up free radicals in the body which have a serious effect on all kinds of metabolic processes. Cider is said to be at least as good in this respect as red wine.

But apple cider vinegar has also been known for generations to be an excellent medicine for all kinds of ailments from increased blood pressure to gout, and for that reason we include a recipe of how to make this from your brews.

Cider is an ancient drink, possibly predating the Romans, but certainly was produced in great quantity by them. The Romans were interested in improving the cultivation of apples, and they took their tree stock around Europe on their conquests; in the end, the brewing of cider became endemic. It is perhaps a northern European drink over any other, but there are still cider makers in Spain, Portugal and Italy as well as the UK and France.

In the UK, cider drinking, though probably a very ancient practice, came to the fore after the Norman conquest, when many orchards were laid down specifically for its manufacture. This was particularly so on the west coast of England, where climate and soil together were most favourable for the growing of apples. But it wasn't just the West Country which had a monopoly of apple growing. At one time every county had its own apple varieties, and often more than one or two. Although many of these varieties have now been lost, there are groups of dedicated people on the search to bring back apples long forgotten.

The remotest part of Wales, the Lleyn Peninsula, is tipped by the even lonelier island of Bardsey. On it is a gnarled apple tree that is 1,000 years old; all that remains of an orchard tended by monks at the turn of the first millennium. Nearby, in a cave, are graves supposed to be those of King Arthur and Merlin. Avalon was said to be filled with apple trees and its name derived from the Welsh, Afal.

The oldest apple with a name is the Pearmain, which dates from some 200 years later than the Bardsey tree, and it's still eaten today. Apple names have now become part of the language. For example, the Costard apple gave its name to the 'costermongers' of London, who sold them on trays. Throughout medieval times apples were developed to suit local climates. The Georgian period saw an explosion of apple varieties: twelve thousand varieties represented almost one recognisable type per village.

UNDERSTANDING APPLES FOR CIDER

It is possible to make cider from any apples, but it is good to understand the properties of apples before embarking on a home cider making career.

Apples come in three varieties: sweet, bittersweet and bittersharp. The difference between them relates to the sugar content, the acidity and the amount of tannin compounds to be found.

Sweet apples have reasonably high sugar content but little in the way of acidity or tannin. Perhaps the most well-known types of sweet apples are the russet family and some of the pippin family, though there are, as you would imagine, a fair number of other varieties.

These are the blandest of all the apples, and are used for adding volume to the cider, diluting the other types.

Bittersweet apples have sweetness but are also high in tannins. This gives a number of flavours to the cider, reminiscent of earthiness and hedgerows. Apples with a lot of tannin include Somerset Red and Tramlett's Bitter. Bittersweet apples are what give cider its flavour, for the most part – being rich and full bodied.

Bittersharp apples are high in tannin and acidity and are full bodied in flavour. They include Royal Pearmain and Cox's Pomona.

You need a good mix of flavours in your cider, and historically most ciders are made from an equal mixture of sweet, bittersweet and bittersharp apples. The truth is, however, as a home cider maker you have little choice unless you grow specific varieties of tree. The full range of varieties of English apples is never going to be available in the supermarkets, and so you have to box clever when making your own.

Crab apples and cider

If you grow apples in the garden these are likely to be sweet apples, which are very high in sugar but low in tannin. However, you can beef up your mix by using crab apples, which grow in hedgerows, or can be bought very cheaply. The crab apple is very high in tannin and if you have a 10% crab apple content in your mix, this will suffice.

Bramley apples are great for cider makers, and will add acidity to your mix. You can make an excellent cider at home from a combination of 10% crab, 30% Bramley and the rest whatever you have in the garden.

MAKING YOUR CIDER SWEET OR DRY

The craft of cider making is just as demanding and exact as the production of wine. If you have a crab apple content of 10% in your mix, then varying the proportions of acid and sweet apples will have noticeable effects on the final product. Sharp, dry cider has a higher proportion of acid apples, and sweet cider has a higher proportion of sweet apples. It is possible to create a dry cider from sweet apples, using a wine yeast instead of natural yeasts and then fermenting for a long time. However, most of us are content to drink a rich cider from our own apples.

Some people add artificial sweetener to their cider. This is to add sweetness that will not ferment away in the fermenting vessel.

TRADITIONAL SMALL-SCALE CIDER MAKING

Apart from the strange goings on in the orchards, where grown men dress up in terrible clothes and utter oaths and undertake strange rituals for the sake of the apple harvest, traditional cider making is much the same wherever you go.

Cider Day is when the community press is used to prepare the apple juice, and people bring their bagged apples to be milled and pressed, releasing the juice which is placed in barrels for natural fermentation.

An apple miller is a hand-cranked machine – though motor-driven ones do exist too – into which whole apples are placed to be chopped up into smaller pieces, each soft enough to be easily pressed. Huge pressure would be needed to juice a whole apple, but when milled the apples can be pressed comparatively easily.

The press itself is usually a wooden affair with a great, hand carved wooden screw and a long branch to turn it. The apples are laid on the press in moulds, a few centimetres high, and are wrapped in washed hessian sacking. When one mould is filled the hessian is gathered around and another mould is added on top. This is repeated until the press is full and a pressure plate, known as a follower, is placed inside the top-most mould.

The men then take it in turn to turn the screw, pressing the life out of the harvest, as it trickles into the waiting barrels.

The barrels are the most important part of the process. An old sherry barrel is probably the best, but port and whisky barrels have been used – but not beer. The juice is poured into the barrel and the barrel is capped, to be stored for a year. Natural yeasts in the apples ferment the sugar and a year later you should have a barrel of cider – though it wasn't always as simple as that.

The solid block of dry apples that was left behind, now known as cheese, was broken up and fed to the pigs, though these days this doesn't happen at all.

Cider Day was also an opportunity for the old boys to bring their cider out from the previous year to be consumed while the current year's was still in preparation. It was a matter of great pride, and the state of the cider was so very important. Of course, as the day wore on . . .

Scrumpy

Windfall apples are known as scrumps, and scrumpy was the cider made from them. Scrumpy used to be cloudy, and sometimes, but rarely, a little vinegary. It would have varying flavours depending how 'off' the apples were and how easily the juice was settled and fermented.

Today the term is used in a marketing sense, often for cheap cider, to give it an authentic appeal, or for very expensive cider to mark it out as a natural product.

MAKING ROUGH CIDER

One of the best pieces of equipment I have ever bought is a bucket pulper. I started – probably like everyone else does – using my tiny food processor. The apple wouldn't fit in and I inevitably cut my fingers chopping the apples so they would fit in the bucket. Then I bought a pulpmaster, and the job became very much easier. Essentially the pulpmaster is a big bucket with a hole in the lid, through which a knife is turned using an electric drill (which you provide yourself).

This makes pulping the apples very straightforward, and you get quite a lot of juice in the bucket. I have found it better to pulse the drill – just as I would have done with the food processor. If you're over eager with it, you end up making soup, which then leads to excessive oxidation and cider that doesn't clear properly.

Ideally you need to produce pieces of apple that are about the size of a pea, which are easy to press to get the juice out.

Make sure you get the obvious bits of apple branches off the fruit before you pulp it, but the odd leaf or so doesn't really matter. This way, should you be using natural yeast to ferment the liquor, you will keep the amount of 'bad' yeast to a minimum, because there are more of these yeasts on the leaves and branches.

Needless to say, everything should be sterile before use – even if the apples aren't – and you should be clean yourself.

One crop I used for cider was a bucket full of apples which I was unable to identify. I couldn't work out what they were for – they were already in the garden, on a huge rambling tree with loads of fruit. They looked like Worcesters, but I still don't really know.

I added another bucket of Bramleys and a pan full of crab apples made up the rest of the mix. Between them they produced well over a bucketful of juice which fitted nicely into two demijohns.

Campden tablets

You may have heard stories of cattle getting drunk on old grapes in vineyards, or pigs eating fermenting apples in orchards. The natural world is covered with microbes, many of which are yeasts of one form or another. Apples tend to have their fair share of 'natural' yeasts, which have the ability to produce alcohol just like wine or beer yeast.

The problem is that you cannot be sure what else is in there too. As apples are full of juice and this is mostly sugar, you are quite likely to have a number of rapidly growing microbes in the mix.

So, for my rough cider, I add a Campden tablet to each demijohn to get rid of any errant microbes. This will also kill the yeast that is present, so you'll need to add in some more – a teaspoon of white wine yeast can be used here.

The demijohns are stored at 18°C and within a few days they are bubbling away.

Racking

This is the process of removing the cider off the lees, which is mainly dead yeast, but in the case of cider there can also be apple debris in it too.

Apples, and more so pears, have woody cells in their flesh called sclereids. These float about in the liquid and take a long time to settle.

Having racked the cider off the lees into another sterile demijohn, store it on a stone floor to allow the contents to settle and then rack again. You can, should you like cider with no fizz, give the bottle a shake to release the carbon dioxide in an alcoholic haze – try not to sniff at it, you'll only want to drink the cider!

Without the carbon dioxide dissolved in the bottle the sediment clears more quickly, but personally, I prefer the fizz. You can rack the cider a couple of times more if you want to, although I usually only do it once more myself.

Stopping fermentation

Add a Campden tablet to each demijohn to finally stop the fermentation by killing the yeast. We do not want any secondary fermentation in the demijohn or the bottle.

Maturing your cider

Cider very definitely improves with age, and if you bottle it and store it in a cool room any final sediment will be sticking to the bottom of the bottle. Your cider should be at its best in 3 months.

Light induced oxidation

Cider deteriorates in the light, so use green or brown bottles unless the cider is to be drunk fairly quickly – say within 6 weeks. Traditionally cider is stored in barrels or in earthenware jars holding a gallon of cider.

CHEATING APPLE WINE

Also known as Turbo Cider, this is really easy to make. Actually you can make a decent wine, or a really healthy boozy drink (who cares about an oxymoron?) like cranberry wine, with any kind of juice from the shops. It is remarkable how many people make this stuff.

Whenever there is a special offer on apple juice, we buy 5 litres. Sometimes you can get this for £2.50, but make sure there are no preservatives in it which will otherwise kill the yeast. If there are preservatives in it, simply boil the liquid for 20 minutes and this will remove most of them.

Pour the liquid into a demijohn and add about 300 g honey, which adds a little extra sugar and a warm flavour. The juice of a lemon adds a little extra acidity. Give the demijohn a really good shaking so all the honey is evenly and completely mixed before adding the yeast.

Add a teaspoon of white wine yeast and set the demijohn in a warm room so it attains 18–21°C fairly quickly. I stand it on a tray to avoid spillages which sometimes can happen, depending on the type of honey.

When the bubbles stop, rack the liquid in the normal manner, possibly twice over and then bottle it. With this brew I do shake the liquid between racking, in order to get a still, dry, apple wine.

MORE COMPLEX CIDER RECIPES

There are lots of cider recipes out there, though the fundamental idea is really just fermented apple juice. However, there are additives and other fruits that make some fine ciders.

Using pectic enzymes

The sweeter apples are high in pectin, which makes them great for jam, but not for straining. When you pulp your apples the pectin escapes from the cells and is turned into a gel by enzymes in the apple. This clogs up the muslin and makes it difficult to strain the liquid from the pulp. It also makes the cider cloudy.

Use a pectic enzyme, such as pectolase, which converts all the pectin overnight. For the correct dosage, make sure you read the instructions on the packet – take care not to exceed the specified amount. Usually, one teaspoon per gallon is required, but do follow the instructions carefully every time. The enzyme will convert all the pectin in the fruit, making pressing easier and giving a clearer cider.

MAKING CIDER USING THE FREEZER

This is another version of turbo cider. Turbo cider is essentially a quick and easy way to make apple wine in small quantities. It is called turbo because it is quick and easy, no other reason. It is not particularly high in alcohol, and some people add sugar to it. If you must, and bear in mind my warning at the beginning that cider doesn't have added sugar in it, add up to 250 g of ordinary sucrose.

This cider is made using a simple collection of apples stored in the freezer. Freezing is really good for getting juice out without bashing the flesh around too much. When water freezes it expands as the crystals of ice form. As the crystals grow inside the apple, they break the cell walls. The juice therefore is released more readily when the apple thaws out.

Ingredients
To make 4.5 litres:

10 kg apples
1 sachet (teaspoon) champagne yeast

Have ready a sterile bucket, demijohn, bung and airlock

Method
- Essentially, you simply need to collect your apples and freeze them. Make sure they are really frozen hard for at least 24 hours and then put them in a single sterile bucket to thaw.
- Cut, bash and mash the apples until they are pressable and then extract the juice.
- Ten kilos of apples will give you just 4.5 litres of juice, and you should add a Campden tablet to the juice to get rid of any unwanted microbes.
- Leave overnight in a demijohn, then add your yeast, and add an airlock.
- Place on a stone floor and rack off when the bubbles stop.
- In order to clear it fully, shake the cider to remove the carbon dioxide, and then store again on the stone floor. Repeat until clear. You can also add finings to clear it.
- If you add 250 g sugar, you will get a final product that is about 11–12% alcohol, otherwise it will be about 5.5% alcohol.

MORE CIDER RECIPES

Since the basic processes are the same, there is no real need to give step by step instructions for cider making. And since cider is all about the apples, you simply need a list for the basic ingredients.

Bear in mind that you need 10 kilos of apples to get 4.5 litres of juice, with a bit left over for topping up, etc. And if you add a vitamin C tablet, the discolouration of the juice will not be so severe.

Good dry cider

Ingredients

> 50% Bramleys, or sharp apples
> 25% Crab apples
> 25% Worcesters (or sweet apples)
> Champagne yeast

When racking, shake off the carbon dioxide if you prefer flat cider, or leave it if you prefer it sparkling. For sparkling cider you will also need to use finings.

Simple dry cider

Ingredients

> 50% sharp apples
> 50% sweet apples – a mixture of varieties is a good idea
> Champagne yeast

Simple sweet cider

Ingredients

75% sweet apples – try Cox's Pippin
25% Bramley
White wine yeast

FRUITED CIDERS

These are becoming more popular, and since they are so terribly expensive in the shops, making them from the garden is a bonus, and it's also very easy.

You could, I suppose, though I have never tried it myself, make a fruit cider by adding fruit juice to your apples. This would not actually give completely satisfactory results because if you use whole fruit the yeasts from the skins of the fruit act on various complex sugars to create a better brew. However, it might be worth trying if you want to see if you would like a blackcurrant cider, and so on.

The type of drink you create will have characteristics similar to those described for cider, for bitterness and so on. So, adding blackcurrant juice for example, will replace some of the sweet apple portion. Adding gooseberry would replace some of the crab apple and so on.

Blackcurrant cider

There are two ways of making this cider: you can add blackcurrants to the original ingredients, and this has to be the best way; or you can add a carton of blackcurrant juice.

Ingredients

To make 22.5 litres:

25 kg Bramleys (or sharp apples)
15 kg Cox's Pippin (or sweet apples)
5 kg blackcurrants
Juice of 4 lemons
Champagne yeast

Have ready a sterile fermentation vessel and airlock

Method

- Simply pulp and press the apples to provide the juice, and then crush the blackcurrants. Combine the juices and add one Campden tablet per litre of juice. Leave for 24 hours.
- Transfer to a fermenting vessel, add the yeast, and fit an airlock.
- The cider will be fermented out in about 10 days and you should rack off and bottle in the normal way (see instructions on page 44).
- If you are going to simply add blackcurrant juice, then pulp and press your apples and make up to 22.5 litres with blackcurrant juice.

MAKING PERRY

Perry is cider made from pears and is a huge, and somewhat complex, series of procedures. Everything said for apple cider is also true for perry, though there are two very significant differences.

Pears have a larger number of woody cells – called sclereids, in the fruit. So perry can be harder to clear than cider. The second is that pears have a much higher acidity of a kind that can be very sharp. Malic acid is particularly bitter and in the making of good perry it is fermented in the bottles during maturation.

The malic acid is converted to lactic acid in the bottles by bacteria already present in the pear juice. It is important that the perry is left to mature in the bottle for a good three months to be sure of a smooth, sweet drink. This fermentation also provides carbon dioxide, and consequently, perry is a lot like champagne.

Babycham is just such a drink, which was very popular in the 1950s. Whenever we make perry we often call it 'babysham' by way of reverence.

Campden tablets

You might be thinking that, if there needs to be a bacterial fermentation in the bottle, will this be killed off by the Campden tablets? Well, yes it will, but you should still use Campden tablets nonetheless. If you use only 1 tablet for 6 litres of perry, this should leave enough bacteria to do the job while killing off the wild yeasts.

Pears for perry making

For home perry making the selection of fruit doesn't really matter that much – it is so exciting making your own perry from your own fruit! However, the same applies to pears as apples, in that there are sweet, bittersweet and bittersharp pears. Professional perry manufacturers use the same combinations to create different types of perry.

Sweet pear varieties include:

- Barnet

- Ducksbarn

- Merrylegs

Bitterssweet pear varieties include:

- Harley Gum
- Thurston's Red

Bittersharp varieties include:

- Barland
- Rock
- Teddington Green
- Or you can use pectic enzyme

But for making your own perry, the variety 'Conference' will do just fine.

Simple perry ('babycham')

Collect about 25 kg pears – I have found this to be three to four trees worth of pears. Collect them gently, and store them for a week to soften a little. Discard any that are damaged and bruised.

Chop and press your fruit – you should get about 10–12 litres of juice.

Perry making is more complex than cider making in that you need to test the pH before you start. You can buy pH strips (what we used to call Litmus paper at school). You simply dip the paper in a sample and compare the colour change against a printed chart. Industrial producers use an electronic meter. Your juice should be no lower than pH 3.6 and no higher than pH 4. You should get your juice to pH 4 by adding precipitated chalk, a teaspoon at a time. Mix well and retest.

Add 1 Campden tablet for every 6 litres of juice, then transfer to a fermenting vessel and leave for 24 hours. Add the appropriate amount of pectic enzyme. Pitch your yeast and leave to ferment with an airlock in place.

FINAL GRAVITY

You need to stop the fermentation at 1020 final gravity, regardless of what you started at. Actually I never measure it to start with – but I always stop at 1020. This is because the sugars in pears include sorbitol – which is not fermentable.

You stop the fermentation by adding one Campden tablet for every 6 litres of perry. Wait 24 hours before you rack off, and then bottle in the usual way and leave to mature for at least 3 months.

Rough perry

This recipe makes about 10 litres, so spread the fermenting over two demijohns.

Ingredients

10 kg pears
10 kg apples
500 g white sucrose (ordinary sugar)
Pectic enzyme
Champagne yeast

Have ready a sterile fermenting bin, two demijohns, bungs and airlocks

Method

- Keep the pears for at least 24 hours before using and discard any rotten ones. Pears often go bad from the inside – so keep an eye on your stock.
- Cut and crush the juice out of the apples and pears and transfer to a bin. This quantity should give you about 10 litres of juice. Add pectolase or another pectic enzyme to this liquid. Leave overnight.
- Add 2 Campden tablets. Stand for 24 hours.
- Add the sugar – note we are using ordinary white sucrose, which works quite well in this recipe, better than brewing sugar I find.
- Pitch your yeast, then add an airlock and let it ferment out. Because this recipe contains half apples you needn't worry about stopping the fermentation at 1020.
- Rack to clear the perry, and then bottle in good quality bottles (see instructions on page 44).

CHAPTER 9

MAKING ROOT BEER, GINGER BEER AND SMALL BEER

This is not the kind of root beer the Americans drink (although that in itself is very nice – made from the sassafras tree), but is a kit beer flavoured also with various roots. In hard times, people would not throw out the liquor from boiling vegetables, but incorporate it in how they cooked, or do something else with it. I have also included some vegetable wines in this chapter because they show you how the juice of various roots and other ingredients are changed in the brewing process.

In Victorian times in particular, cabbage water and carrot water, turnip water and other liquors were used to make up the wort liquid and consequently any goodness dissolved in the water was consumed rather than being poured away.

I have tried this with carrots and turnips, but not parsnips, which for me add a flavour that is too aromatic for consumption. (I managed a sip or two of a friend's parsnip beer once, but not the whole pint!)

CARROT BEER

Ingredients

1 pale ale or bitter kit
2 kg carrots (chopped into 1 cm pieces)
500 g sugar (or whatever the kit instructions ask for)

Have ready a sterile fermentation vessel, muslin bag and airlock

Method
- Take 2 kilos of carrots, chopped quite small – into about 1 cm pieces – and boil for 15 minutes in 2 litres of water.
- Strain this through a muslin cloth into your wort, then make up to 22.5 litres with cold water. It is a good idea to use pale malt as a sugar supply for this brew. The beer has a really excellent flavour, and a good head.
- Follow the instructions for the kit (see also Chapter 3).

CARROT WINE

This gives a dry, white wine. Use older carrots for the best flavour; new season carrots are too light in taste.

Ingredients

2 kg carrots
White grape juice to top up the demijohn (this will depend on the amount of water you use to boil the carrots – I try to boil in 1.5 litres, but there is always wastage)

900 g white sugar
1 crushed vitamin C tablet mixed with 1 dessertspoon warm water
1 tsp yeast nutrient (if not already contained in the yeast compound)
Yeast, as directed on the packet

Have ready a sterile demijohn, bung and airlock

Method

- Wash and scrub the carrots if necessary. Do not peel them. Cut them into slices and place in a pan with sufficient boiling water to cover with 2 cm to spare.
- Bring to the boil, then reduce the heat and simmer for 20–25 minutes or until very tender.
- Strain the liquid into a large jug or bowl and discard or eat the pulp. (You can add it to soups, as it doesn't require any more cooking, just heating up.)
- Pour the carrot liquor into a pan and stir in the sugar. Heat and stir until all the sugar has dissolved.
- Leave to cool to about 20°C and then pour into a demijohn.
- Add the vitamin C tablet and nutrient, if using, then top up the demijohn with the grape juice, leaving a little to help mix the yeast into the solution.
- Add the correct amount of yeast for the amount of liquid, pouring in the rest of the grape juice to swill the yeast down.
- Fit with an airlock, containing a little cooled boiled water, add the bung and leave in a warm place until it starts to ferment. The airlock will start to pop regularly when fermentation is underway.
- Leave to ferment for about 10–15 days or until the popping has stopped completely.
- Rack the wine off into another sterile demijohn, fitted with an airlock as before, and leave in a cooler place. Shake the demijohn

well to expel as much of the carbon dioxide as possible. Do this after each change of demijohn. After each racking, top up with a little grape juice if the level of the wine reduces.

- When the sediment has appeared at the bottom, rack off once more. Leave for two weeks, then siphon into sterile bottles and cork immediately. Dry the bottles and label with the type of wine and date bottled. Leave for at least three months before drinking. Leaving for six months makes a fuller very well-flavoured dry white wine.

POTATO BEER

Potatoes are full of starch, which gives us a way of enhancing beer if we add potatoes to the grain malts in the mashing time. However, potatoes come in different varieties and each has their own quality. I prefer to use new potatoes for this – something with a bit of bite. I find old potatoes produce a beer that never clears – and the new potato can be quite cloudy too!

Ingredients
To make 22.5 litres:

2.5 kg crushed pale malt
1 kg new potatoes, chopped small
125 g crystal malt
100 g Goldings hops
Top fermenting beer yeast

Have ready a sterile fermenting vessel, muslin bag and airlock

Method
- Chop the potatoes into 1 cm cubes – don't bother to peel, but do give them a wash. Bring the potatoes to the boil in a pan and

then allow to cool – use the liquid in the wort once cool. Pop the potatoes in a muslin bag to separate them from the rest of the mash.

- Mash the grains and the potatoes in 5 litres of water with the crystal malt for an hour at 60°C, and then add the hops. Remove the potatoes and drain as much of the liquid from them as you can.
- Bring to the boil and then allow to cool before filtering into another vessel. Make up to 22.5 litres with cold water.
- Add the yeast and over the course of a week remove any foam that appears before fitting an airlock – or transferring to another vessel with an airlock fitted.
- Ten days later you can clear the beer with finings and then rack off into another vessel.
- Before bottling, prime the beer. That is, add sugar for a secondary fermentation in the bottle. Use 125 g brewing sugar in a cup of warm water.
- Bottle (see instructions on page 44) and then store for at least a month.

POTATO WINE

This produces a medium to sweet wine. If after the last fermentation the wine is too dry, add a small can of grape concentrate to the demijohn before bottling.

Ingredients

3 kg potatoes (old ones)
1.2 kg white sugar, or if you would like a deep golden finish to the wine use brown sugar (demerara is ideal)
200 ml of strong cold tea (I use 3 tea bags in the boiling water and leave them to go cold before removing)

2 litres white grape juice
Cool boiled water for topping up
Yeast

Have ready a sterile demijohn, bung and airlock

Method

- Wash and scrub the skins of the potatoes, but do not peel. Slice thinly and place in a pan. Pour over sufficient cold water to cover with 2 cm to spare.
- Bring to the boil and simmer for 10 minutes, or until just tender but not falling into the water.
- Strain the liquor into a large jug and pour back into a clean pan.
- Add the sugar and heat gently whilst stirring until all the sugar has dissolved.
- Allow to cool a little before pouring into the demijohn.
- Top up with the grape juice and the cold tea, then top up to the shoulder of the demijohn with cooled boiled water.
- Add the yeast as directed on the pack and rinse down with a little extra water.
- Fit an airlock and allow the wine to ferment in a warm place for 24 hours.
- Remove to a place where it is at room temperature out of direct sunlight and leave to ferment for 10–12 days.
- Rack off into another sterile demijohn when fermentation has stopped. Shake the demijohn to get rid of the carbon dioxide. Do this after each racking. Top up with a little grape juice if necessary.
- As there is some starchy sediment with this type of wine, rack off at least twice more, leaving a week between each change, then clear the wine with a Campden tablet in the final racking.
- Leave to completely clear before bottling and labelling (see instructions on page 44).

Leave this to mature for at least 7–8 months before drinking. The optimum time for leaving this wine to mature is 12 months; it really does improve with age. Try drinking one after 7 months and then one after 12 months to see the difference.

MIXED-ROOT DRY WHITE WINE

This makes a dry, light flavoured wine that reminds me of a dry Martini. It's included here because it is really gorgeous, though yes, it's not beer!

Ingredients

700 g carrots
700 g parsnips
700 g turnips
1 kg sugar
2 litres white grape juice
150 ml cold, light-strength tea
Yeast
Cooled boiled water

Have ready a sterile demijohn, bung and airlock

Method

- Wash and scrub all the vegetables but do not peel. Slice them thinly and place in a pan with enough warm water to cover them, with 2 cm to spare, then bring to the boil and simmer for 20 minutes until tender.
- Strain the liquor into a large jug or bowl and place back in a clean pan over a low heat.
- Stir in the sugar, and continue stirring until the sugar has dissolved.

- Allow to cool slightly, then pour into the demijohn. Add the cold tea.
- Add the grape juice and top up with cool boiled water.
- Add the yeast and wash down with a little extra water.
- Fit an airlock and leave in a warm place to ferment.
- After 24 hours, move to room temperature and leave to ferment for about 10–12 days.
- Rack off the wine into a clean, sterile demijohn, shaking well to expel as much of the carbon dioxide as possible. Then leave to settle for one week.
- Rack off again into a sterile demijohn, topping up with cool boiled water if necessary. Shake well and fit an airlock, then leave to settle for one more week.
- The wine should be beginning to clear now. Add a Campden tablet and leave for three more days.
- It should be ready to bottle now (see instructions on page 44). If it is still a little cloudy leave for two more days, then bottle. To give the wine a fuller taste, allow it to oxidise slightly by leaving off the corks or lids for 30 minutes before sealing the lids.
- Leave to mature for at least six months before drinking. This makes a great aperitif before a meal.

This wine method can be made using just parsnips if you wish – the flavour will be slightly fragrant and almost sherry-like. Use only 1 litre of grape juice and top up with cool boiled water.

GINGER BEER

The best ginger beer in the world was made in the UK. Granted, this isn't a hop/barley beer, but it is beer, and came in two forms – alcoholic and non-alcoholic, though the majority of alcoholic ginger beers never caught on. Interestingly, at the time of writing, there is a product on the market purporting to be an original alcoholic ginger beer, but as they say, there is nothing new under the sun!

The great thing about ginger beer – good alcoholic ginger beer – is that it's like elderflower champagne: explosive. You need to reduce the pressure in the bottles, and therefore I'd use good quality PET bottles that I could unscrew.

Ingredients
To make 22.5 litres:

1 kg ginger cut into 1 cm cubes
1 tsp cream of tartar
Juice of 6 lemons
2 kg brewing sugar
A packet of champagne yeast

Have ready a sterile fermentation vessel, muslin bag and airlock

Method
- Add the ginger, lemon juice and cream of tartar to about 4 litres of water and boil for 20 minutes.
- Strain into another pan and then dissolve the sugar in the hot liquid.
- Make up to 22.5 litres by adding cold water to your fermenting vessel – a keg is best for this. Check the temperature is in the range between 18 and 21°C. Pitch your yeast and add an airlock.
- Allow to ferment for 7–10 days and then rack off. Once you have racked your beer, bottle it immediately (see instructions on page 44).
- Release the gas after a few days and then consume after another fortnight.

SMALL BEER

This was made from the second mashing of the barley after the first wort had been taken off. To be honest, I can't think of a reason why you would want to make it these days – essentially the remaining sugars in the wort are now washed into the wort of the first batch.

Also, we do not make beer at home in the same quantities we used to when small beer was used as the common drink of the day. Water could never be trusted to be safe, so small beer was drunk. At the turn of the 18th century, people would brew 100–150 litres at a time, and the same of small beer. When you only brew 22.5 litres, there are not enough residual sugars and flavours left in the mash to make another batch of beer.

There are a lot of recipes from a couple of hundred years ago for small beer, but they are of a different type, using molasses instead of barley.

George Washington's small beer

This is an approximation because the quantities he used were much larger than we now brew. It is a molasses brew with barley too.

Ingredients
To make 22.5 litres:

2 kg pale malt extract
500 g molasses
Beer yeast

Have ready a sterile fermentation vessel, muslin bag and airlock

Method

- Boil the malt for 30 minutes and then add the molasses. Boil for a further 15 minutes to dissolve and then strain into a fermenting vessel having allowed it to cool.
- Add water to make 22.5 litres and check the temperature.
- If it is in the range between 18 and 21°C then pitch your yeast.
- Add an airlock after a couple of days, and then allow it to ferment for a week.
- Rack the beer when the bubbles slow to less than one a minute and then bottle (see instructions on page 44).

CHAPTER 10

MAKING TRUE HOME BREW

There are a growing number of people who are brewing home-brew beer and cider from very first principles – i.e. they are growing their own barley and hops. Of course, the main reason why people make cider is they have apple trees. For me it started with the inheritance of an old apple tree that provided a lot of juice. From there it is only a short step to growing your own apples just for cider making – well, I suppose a few apple pies are good too!

Growing all the ingredients you need is neither onerous nor expensive. If you live in a warm area of the UK you can grow hops quite well, and anyone with an allotment can grow barley, harvest it and thresh it over the back of a chair. A quarter of an average allotment given over to barley will give you enough for 20 gallons of beer, and I underestimated the sums!

GROWING HOPS

The hop, *Humulus lupulus*, is a vine that is reasonably frost hardy, though will not withstand really severe frosts that are prolonged. It starts its growth in April and produces flowers in August, which then have to be prepared for use in beer making.

If you can grow potatoes, then you should be able to grow hops, although they are very different crops in reality. Essentially, though, they have the same needs.

How to buy hops to grow

Hops are sold as rhizomes which are delivered in late autumn/winter. You should plant them straight away. There are lots of hop suppliers, but be sure you buy beer quality hops because many domestic hops are produced for health and decorative uses.

Preparing the land

You need to dig over the soil a few months before you are going to introduce your hops, which probably means sometime in August, since it is best to put hops in the ground in the winter when they are dormant.

You can buy rhizomes from a number of suppliers, and they need to be planted in nutrient rich soil, with plenty of very rich compost, about 45 cm deep. The soil should be free draining – they don't like wet roots and do best in a sunny position, against a south-facing wall.

They appear above the ground in April and May. I cover them if there is going to be a late frost – where possible, using bubble wrap.

A regular (weekly) feeding with a good, all-purpose fertiliser will keep them growing skyward. Fix some hooks at the top of the roof and run a rope from the ground, through the hook and back again. The hop will climb this and you can unhook the rope to collect the hop flowers.

Harvesting your crop

The flowers should be harvested in late August – when the flowers seem to be papery and drying. Leave the vine to grow after flowering until it dies back naturally, but cut it down when it starts to look scruffy.

Preparing the hops

Dry the hops in a desiccator or a very, very low oven. This takes many hours, and they should have a very papery feel to them. If you are able to vacuum seal them then all the better, otherwise, keep them in an airtight container.

About four plants will provide you with all the hops you are ever going to need. You can buy the favourite varieties too, Fuggles, Goldings and so on.

Winter preparation

You should make sure that the plants are not bothered by frost in the winter. Cover the spot where the rhizome lies with leaf mould, then a thick layer of straw, topping this with soil to secure. In the spring, take the straw away and replace it with compost.

GROWING BARLEY

Unlike growing hops (which is fun, you can definitely get an easy crop in a reasonable length of time, and the process is full of interest and developing skill), there is not much benefit to growing your own barley except that you can do it, and you can get a great yield and all but free beer.

Nothing is easier than growing barley. You need a good seedbed, produced by hoeing, or perhaps rotovating the soil. Then rake it over and broadcast the seed liberally. Rake over again and leave it. There is nothing to do to it!

You can sow in September, where it will germinate and then stop as the cold arrives, to start growing again in spring. Alternatively you can sow in spring. Either way, about 60–70 days after the first spring growth, you get a crop.

Harvesting and threshing

Cut the barley with a sickle, which is easy if you only have half an allotment's worth, and tie an armful into a sheaf with string. Leave these stood up to dry, and you can then start the job of threshing a week later.

To thresh your barley, place a chair on a sheet and then bash the seed out of the barley. On the sheet there will be seeds, and husks which you winnow away – to do this, get the four corners of the sheet and toss the barley lightly into the air – all the non-grain bits will blow away.

Home malting

This is actually not that easy to do. You might just want to roast the grains and use them with other malts that you buy.

Fill a bucket with barley and add water to it. Leave for two hours then filter out the seeds. Pop them on a tray to dry for a few hours and then re-steep. Repeat this process a couple more times and then prepare for germination. You should start to have the beginnings of root growth peeping out.

Germination

Lay the barley about in layers of about 1 cm thickness on trays. The grains need to be at about 18°C, and you are going to have to keep them at this temperature. The grains get hot, so turn them over twice a day. Open up a seed and you will see a small leaf growing inside the white endosperm. When this has grown to about ⅔ the size of the seed the barley is ready.

The barley has to be dried at 30°C – not an easy job. Finding a warm spot near the greenhouse door is as good as anywhere – but keep the birds off!

Finally, shake the malted, dry, barley around a colander to knock the roots off.

Roasting the barley

As it is, in its raw state, you can use the barley for light beers, lager, pale ale, bitter and so on.

You can roast it – although it's actually best to put under a grill on trays, until it attains the colour you prefer. Keep your eyes on it though – it burns easily and you will be brewing nothing but stout and Guinness if you let it go too far.

GROWING APPLES

Which variety to grow

You can find an apple to suit you; there are so many varieties! They come in four types; cookers, eaters, crab (for making jelly, and wine for the brave) and cider apples. Cider apples are medium-sweet, cooking apples are less sweet. Crab apples can be very bitter and need a lot of sugar adding to them, but are very rich in pectin for making jelly. And of course, eating apples are completely deliciously sweet. We have already mentioned the varieties needed for good cider production (see pages 114–15).

Some older varieties are not self-fertile, and you need more than one tree. Modern varieties – actually those younger than around 80 years old – are often self-fertile. You can buy apples on dwarfing rootstocks so they fit on the patio, growing vertically up and down, or you can grow them on free roots that will allow a huge plant to develop. You can get every size and shape of tree, though it is probably best to buy apples on medium rootstocks.

How to buy apple trees

Most nurseries sell by mail order and most garden centres keep a reasonable stock. Look for a sturdy, well-pruned plant that is at least a year old. All except the most dwarfed trees will be around four to five feet tall. In the winter months, from November onwards they will be bare rooted. In the spring and summer they will be sold in pots. Before you buy, ask about how they will be delivered and their quality and what special requirements they might have.

Planting patio apples

Patio apples need a 45 cm pot, the bottom few centimetres of which should be filled with crocks to help drainage. Use good quality compost and mix it with ordinary soil. Soil alone will do but is more troublesome to remove in the spring to be replaced with fresh nutrient-rich compost. Two problems with patio apples, easily overcome, are that they blow over – so make sure they are sheltered or tied down – and they dry out more easily, so water them. Extra watering leaches nutrients so you will have to feed a little more too.

Planting out

Dig a hole three times as wide as the roots and twice as deep. Fill to one-third the depth with compost or manure. If you are using manure, make sure it is really well rotted.

Hold the plant into position so the graft mark can be seen at ground level and backfill with soil. Firm in well with your boot and then support the young tree with a sturdy stake.

Caring for your apple trees

Make sure the plant is not dry, but don't panic as nothing happens until late spring, when buds burst into life. Flowers may drop, fruit may drop, the plant may take a whole year to establish, and there might not be much in the way of fruit for the next two years. But still don't panic! If you feed and care for it in the early stages your apple tree will be fruitful for the next 20 years.

Pruning

With a new tree, in the first winter, you will need to reduce it by a third. There is usually only a single branch. If there is more than one, reduce each of the branches by a third. Always cut just above an outward-facing bud.

In the following year, do the same to each branch that has formed, and in the next year, repeat and also cut out any branches that are touching each other.

Cut with a slope, so rainwater will run off and not soak into the wood.

Pruning the plant will change the way hormones interact within the plant, resulting in the production of more flowers, and consequently more fruit. Also, it opens out the plant so air can more easily circulate, reducing the likelihood of fungal infections. Where branches touch, there is the obvious probability that the contact will lead to damage, which in turn might lead to infection, so cutting out touching branches is important.

Moist soil and dry feet

Most apple trees need water and like a moist soil. But, contradicting this is the fact that they hate to be stood in water. A clay soil isn't the best for apple trees – it is cold, wet, and there is not much oxygen for the roots. You need a good, rich, sandy loam with plenty of organic matter.

Feeding your apple trees

Feed with a good compost mulch in February rather than spring – this way you will have well-fed trees with nutrients at the roots when they are needed, rather than when the flowers first appear. Don't let the compost touch the stem, but place it in a ring around it.

Should a really sharp frost be forecast – spraying the flowers with a fine mist of water is often an excellent way of preserving the young fruit.

Starting an orchard

Planning starts a full 12 months in advance. Apart from a plan of the plants you want, and working out where to put them (shelter from wind and rain is most important – even more than harsh frosts), you need to buy a tonne of muck and set it down to rot, for a whole year, then incorporate it into the soil.

Always buy new stock for a new orchard – and make sure that it is certified virus free, to avoid bringing in problems. It is also easier to plant new stock, with either bare roots or container-grown root systems, than digging up another apple. You always damage roots when digging up – and you will have disappointments.

Don't forget, the pruning and feeding regime is there for a purpose – it's not just garden messing about. If you just leave them to their own devices you will have weakened plants.

Space your apple trees at least four metres apart and put the space between them down to grass.

BREWING GLOSSARY

Like everything else, in order to explain what is going on in brewing, a whole language has built up. Sometimes it is confusing and even a little odd. Some countries have their own brewing language altogether and this causes even more confusion.

Adjunct
This refers to any sugars in the wort that have not come from malt.

Airlock
A bent tube, usually made from plastic, that allows CO_2 to escape, but stops air or contaminants from coming into the brewing vessel.

Alcohol
The preservative and slightly narcotic group made from the group R–OH where the R could be any organic molecule. It's the OH bit that makes it an alcohol. In beer, cider and wine making the important alcohol is ethanol. Any other alcohol, especially methanol, is quite poisonous.

Alcohol by volume (ABV)
This is the percentage of alcohol as a volume compared to the total volume of liquid. A beer of 5% would have 50 ml alcohol per litre of beer. You calculate this by taking the change of the specific gravity and multiplying by 131.

The readings must be taken at the same temperature – usually a standard 60°F.

Alcohol by weight (ABW)

This is the percentage by weight of alcohol compared to the weight of beer. It is not the same as ABV because alcohol is less dense than water.

Ale

These are beers produced from the Middle Ages onwards that do not have any hops in them. They were often flavoured with herbs. These days you see the word ale on a bottle of beer if it has been brewed at higher temperatures than the common 18–20°C, or if it is high in alcohol.

Amber malt

A roasted light malt that imparts a roasted flavour. It needs to be used with other malts as the enzymes are killed in the roasting.

Amylase

A series of enzymes found in grain seeds (and others for that matter). When the seed takes in water, these enzymes turn starch into sugar and the seed sprouts. In brewing terms, this process produces malt. A malthouse has grain thrown on a floor, often near a fire. The grain, usually barley, is then soaked in water. Just as it begins to sprout, the starch has turned to sugar, which we can then extract to feed our yeast in the brewing process.

Attenuation

This is a measure of how the sugars have been converted into alcohol during the process of fermentation. This is usually calculated by dividing the change in specific gravity by the original specific gravity and a percentage. Most beer is around 70%, although cider can be a lot more.

Barley

The grain from which malt is made and consequently, beer!

Base malt
This is malt that has not been roasted. It has sugar, and amylase. This produces enough enzyme to convert the starch in other grains you add to the mixture to make the wort. It is often called Pale Malt.

Beer
Fermented grain with hops as a flavouring and preservative.

Biscuit malt
This has been toasted, and is lighter than amber malt which has been roasted. It needs base malt to provide the enzymes necessary for conversion of starch.

Bitter
An English beer with lots of hops. It comes in two basic forms, Ordinary, and Best which is stronger.

Bottle capper
A levered machine that crimps the lids on beer bottles.

Brown malt
Malt roasted to become brown. It produces a chocolate-flavoured brown ale.

Campden tablets
A sulphur-based product used in beer and wine making to kill bacteria and inhibit the growth of wild yeasts. Campden tablets are also used towards the end of the brewing process to stop fermentation before all the available sugars are converted by the yeast – hence controlling the amount of sweetness in the final product.

Caramel malt
This is grain that has been malted at a stable temperature, producing some caramelisation in the husk. It is very similar to crystal malt.

Carbon dioxide

This is the gas 'burped' out by the yeast during fermentation. It dissolves in the brewing liquid, but is easily knocked out of solution, and consequently gives beer its fizzing quality.

Chocolate malt

Dark roasted malt giving a chocolate flavour to the beer.

Crystal malt

Barley that has been kept at the optimum temperature so that all of the starch in the seed is converted to sugar. This is then dried. It is the basic sugar based malt.

Dark stout

Like Guinness, this has been brewed with dark roasted malts to impart a roasted flavour.

Doppelbock

This is a strong German ale, so strong that the word is often used as an indication of the strength of some beers and ales – especially in the US.

Dried hops

These can be added to the fermenting liquid to add a hoppy aroma to the beer.

Dried malt extract

This is malt, dried. Simple really. It comes in a variety of forms from light to dark.

Extract brewing

This is a halfway house between kit brewing and using raw materials. The wort is made from extracts produced commercially and put together to make the recipes.

Fermentation
The kind of respiration that turns sugars into alcohol and carbon dioxide.

Final gravity (finishing gravity)
This is the measurement of the 'density' of the brew after all fermentation stops. Used in calculating the percentage of alcohol.

Finings
A substance added to the brew that catches small particles to clear away cloudiness.

Flaked maize
Corn that is heated and crushed between rollers and is used in some recipes. Rather like cornflakes.

Fusel
These are alcohols caused by brewing at too high temperatures. They are the main reason for poor home brew, and give you hangovers as your liver complains about their presence in your blood. They can also be formed by wild yeast.

Grain bag (jam bag)
A bag, often made of muslin, used for steeping grain and other ingredients into wort, usually in extraction brewing. You can also use a jam bag which is finer woven and often made of nylon.

Grist
The dry ingredients often mixed together prior to making a wort.

Growler
A four pint jug for use in making a wort.

Head retention
The term for the length of time a head lasts, which can be increased by adding certain ingredients to the brew.

Head space

The term for the amount of space there is between the top of the brewing liquid and the lid. This should be as short as possible to avoid excess oxidisation. Carbon dioxide builds up in this space to exclude oxygen.

Hops

These are the flowers of a vine-like plant. They give beer its bitter flavour, and preserve it a little too.

Hydrometer

Used for measuring the specific gravity of the brew (i.e. the ratio of the density of the liquid to the density of water), this is a float with a graduated tube and lead weight in the bottom. It is floated in the brew and the reading is proportional to the force it takes to float the tube. The reading is also proportional to the amount of alcohol in the brew.

India Pale Ale (IPA)

When India was part of the British Empire, the gentlemen wanted English beer. This ale was made using a lot of hops, which preserved it on its journey to the subcontinent. It is an example of the preservation of beer with hops.

International Bittering Units (IBU)

The hop aroma comes from what are described as 'alpha acids'. The IBU is the number of milligrams of these acids in a litre of beer.

Isinglass

This is used to clear brews that are cloudy, a kind of finings.

Lager

Beer fermented in cool temperatures using special yeast.

Lauter
This is a way of making beer which separates the wort (the liquid we brew and ferment) from the solid part. This involves the use of a false-bottomed area where the solids are kept.

Lees
Dead yeast and other solid material in the brew, which will spoil the flavour of the brew.

Light malt extract
This is the lightest of the malts you can buy. It is light in flavour too.

Malt
Grain (usually barley) that has been sprouted to release enzymes and start the conversion of starch into sugar. The malted grain is cooled just as it has started to sprout.

Mash
This is the collection of malt, sometimes also other grains, even other substance and plant extracts, mixed with water.

Mash vessel, mash tun
This is the vessel in which the mashing is done. Sometimes this is also used for brewing too, sometimes not. Tun is an ancient term for vessel.

Ordinary bitter
Light beer with low alcohol strength flavoured with hops.

Original gravity
This is the 'density' of the brew before brewing. When subtracted from the final gravity, the only change can be due to the removal of sugar in the wort and the addition of alcohol. Thus difference between the two gives a measure of alcohol content.

Pitching

Pitching the yeast – literally means throwing it into the wort, but be a bit more careful than that.

Porter

This beer comes from black malt, which gets its characteristics from roasting.

Pressing

Extracting the juice from apples (or fruit) in readiness for use.

Priming

When bottling beers, a little sugar is added so a secondary fermentation occurs in the bottle, creating the fizz.

Racking

Siphoning off beer, cider or wine from the solids left behind (lees).

Roasted barley

This is barley grain, not malted, roasted until it is very dark. It is used to create stout.

Small beer

This is beer produced from the mash being rinsed and fermented yielding little alcohol. It was the staple drink of the working poor in pre-industrial times.

Sparging

Rinsing all the sugars out of the grain into the wort.

Yeast

A fungus which turns sugar to alcohol. There are many yeasts for different uses from beer to wine (and cider).

INDEX

alcohol content 28, 31
amber malt 50
apples for cider 114

barley 15, 52
barley wine 101
beer kit 2, 7, 60
beer recipes 32
best beer 20
bitter from extract 77
bitterness 36
black malt 51
bottle cap 27
bottles 26
bottling 44
brewing vessel 21
brown ale 91, 93
brown malt 51

campden tablets 40
capper 27
carbonation 37
carrot beer 132
carrot wine 132
chilli beer 57
chocolate malt 51
cider 112
cleaning 42
crystal malt 49

dark lager 110
demijohn 23
disinfecting 41

easy lager 107

fermentation 13
flaked maize 109
four row barley 16
fruit miller 23
fruited cider 125

ginger beer 138
glossary 151
Guinness 94

home malting 146
homebrew 142
honeyed beer 103
hops 52
hops preserving beer 54
hydrometer 25, 30

IPA 76, 82

keg 46
kriek beer 58

lager 105
lees 3

light pale ale 83

Mackeson 100
malt 48
malt extract 7
mash tun 22
mashing 8
mild beer 87
mixed root wine 137
mulled beer 59
muslin 25

original gravity 31
oxygen 13

paddle 23
pale ale 74
pale ale from extract 80
pale malt 50
perry 126
pilsner malt 51
pitching yeast 66
porter 97
potato beer 134
pressure vessel 21

racking 120
root beer 131

saaz hops 108
scrumpy 118
secondary fermentation 44
sensible drinking 6
simple bitter 55
simple mild 89
six row barley 16
small beer 140
spray malt 50
SRM 36
sterilizing 39, 43
storing bottles 46
stout 96
sugar 14, 30

temperature 12
thermometer 27
tubing 23
turbo wine 121
two row barley 15

vitamin C 13

water 12
wheat beer 84
wort 48

yeast 8